Series / Number 07-069

PRINCIPAL COMPONENTS ANALYSIS

GEORGE H. DUNTEMAN
Research Triangle Institute

SAGE PUBLICATIONS
The International Professional Publishers
Newbury Park   London   New Delhi

For information address:

 SAGE Publications, Inc.
2455 Teller Road
Newbury Park, California 91320
E-mail: order@sagepub.com

SAGE Publications Ltd.
6 Bonhill Street
London EC2A 4PU
United Kingdom

SAGE Publications India Pvt. Ltd.
M-32 Market
Greater Kailash I
New Delhi 110 048 India

International Standard Book Number 0-8039-3104-2

Library of Congress Catalog Card No. 89-063965

96 97 98 99 00 01 13 12 11 10 9 8 7

When citing a university paper, please use the proper form. Remember to cite the correct Sage University Paper series title and include the paper number. One of the following formats can be adapted (depending on the style manual used):

(1) McCutcheon, A. L. (1987). *Latent class analysis* (Sage University Paper series on Quantitative Applications in the Social Sciences, No. 07-064). Newbury Park, CA: Sage.
OR
(2) McCutcheon, A. L. 1987. *Latent class analysis.* Sage University Paper series on Quantitative Applications in the Social Sciences, series no. 07-064. Newbury Park, CA: Sage.

CONTENTS

SERIES EDITOR'S INTRODUCTION*

With principal components analysis a large number of independent variables can be systematically reduced to a smaller, conceptually more coherent set of variables. These "principal components" are a linear combination of the original variables. For example, suppose the analyst has 15 measures of automobile driving ability (taken on 100 randomly selected license applicants). From this data set one principal component variable, perhaps representing General Driving Skill, might be extracted. (Of course, the technique allows the possibility that more than one principal component could be uncovered). The potential efficiency gains from such a data-reduction procedure applied to the independent variables are obvious, and research uses are many. When the researcher has a small sample, a multicollinearity threat, or conceptual uncertainties regarding index construction, the technique has special appeal.

The volume at hand provides a rigorous introduction to principal components analysis, through the use of simple mathematical-geometrical explication and multiple real-world examples. As a teaching device, current crime statistics on the American states are examined from various perspectives. An overriding question here is whether the seven different crime measures can be reduced, perhaps to a single general crime dimension. Other examples are explored, such as the determinants of cross-national differences in educational expenditures, the measurement of satisfaction among army personnel, and the identification of heroin abuse indicators.

Such examples are used to illustrate the search for principal components. As well, they serve as a basis for consideration of such problems as multicollinearity and outliers. Further, principal components is carefully compared to other multivariate techniques. In a sense, it is a special case of factor analysis. (Thus, this volume makes an ideal introduction to the Kim and Mueller factor analysis monographs, Nos. 13 and 14.) However, according to Dr. Dunteman, principal components analysis differs in important ways from factor analysis. He goes on to discuss differences and similarities with discriminant function,

5

canonical correlation, and cluster analysis. Finally, Dunteman's mode of presentation is "flexible." For instance, while he makes use of matrix algebra, its knowledge is not a prerequisite for understanding. Thus, students at different levels, beginning or advanced, will find new material that is accessible.

—*Michael S. Lewis-Beck*
Series Editor

*This volume was initially accepted by the former editors, Richard Niemi and John Sullivan.

PRINCIPAL COMPONENTS ANALYSIS

GEORGE H. DUNTEMAN
Research Triangle Institute

1. INTRODUCTION

Principal components analysis is a statistical technique that linearly transforms an original set of variables into a substantially smaller set of uncorrelated variables that represents most of the information in the original set of variables. Its goal is to reduce the dimensionality of the original data set. A small set of uncorrelated variables is much easier to understand and use in further analyses than a larger set of correlated variables. The idea was originally conceived by Pearson (1901) and independently developed by Hotelling (1933).

The author has attempted to minimize the use of matrix algebra in this paper. Where matrix algebra is used, the author provides, in some instances, definitions of matrix algebra concepts and examples of their use. For a good elementary introduction to matrix algebra, the reader is referred to an earlier paper in this series, Namboodiri's (1984) *Matrix Algebra: An Introduction.* The reader, with little or no knowledge of matrix algebra is encouraged to read this paper in order to obtain the maximum benefit from the present paper.

This book uses numerous real-life examples to illustrate the myriad applications of principal components analysis. If he or she wishes, the reader can devote less attention to the mathematics and focus his or her attention on the applied examples and still learn a great deal about principal components analysis. The reader will see how principal components can enhance our understanding of the structure of a data set composed of a large number of correlated variables. He or she will also see how principal components can be effectively used in conjunction with other multivariate analysis techniques, such as multiple regression analysis and discriminant analysis.

Many times a social science researcher has numerous correlated measures within a particular domain. In order to both simplify and impose some structure on the domain, the researcher would be interested in reducing the number of variables from p to a much smaller set of k derived variables that retain most of the information in the original p variables. For example, an organizational psychologist may have 20 Likert-type items measuring various aspects of job satisfaction (e.g., pay, working conditions, supervision, co-workers, fringe benefits, etc.). There are clearly too many variables to use as independent, intervening, or dependent variables in a subsequent statistical model. If the variables are correlated, and especially if they are highly correlated, then we can linearly transform the p correlated variables into a relatively small set of k uncorrelated variables such that the k derived variables, if considered as independent variables, will maximize the prediction of the original p variables. The k derived variables which maximize the variance accounted for in the original variables are called principal components. If 3 principal components account for most of the variance in the original 20 job satisfaction measures, then we have reduced the dimensionality of our data set from 20 correlated dimensions to 3 uncorrelated dimensions and thus considerably simplified the structure of the job satisfaction variable domain. The aim of principal components analysis is parsimony.

The technique has been applied to virtually every substantive area including biology, medicine, chemistry, meteorology, and geology, as well as the behavioral and social sciences. For example, Morrison (1976) conducted a principal components analysis of a correlation matrix given by Birren and Morrison (1961) for 11 subscales of the Wechsler Adult Intelligence Scale (WAIS) along with age and years of education completed for a sample of 933 white males and females. The goal was to isolate the dimensions underlying the variation in the WAIS subscales and, in addition, to see how age and education were related to these dimensions. Two principal components, the underlying dimensions, accounted for over 62% of the variation in the original 13 variables. The first principal component, which by itself explained over 51% of the total variance in the 13 variables, had high correlations with all 11 WAIS subtests (i.e., .62 to .83) and was interpreted as a measure of general intellectual ability. Education had a correlation of .75 with this dimension. The second principal component, which accounted for 11% of the total variation in the 13 variables, correlated positively with the verbal subtests and negatively with the performance subtests. It was interpreted as a contrast between verbal and performance subtests. People who scored high on this dimension had high verbal scores and low performance scores. Age correlated .80 with this dimension indicating that older people did better on verbal tests than on performance tests, compared with younger people.

The goal of principal components analysis is similar to factor analysis in that both techniques try to explain part of the variation in a set of observed variables on the basis of a few underlying dimensions. There are, however, as discussed in Chapter 8, important differences between the two techniques. Briefly, principal components analysis has no underlying statistical model of the observed variables and focuses on explaining the total variation in the observed variables on the basis of the maximum variance properties of principal components. Factor analysis, on the other hand, has an underlying statistical model that partitions the total variance into common and unique variance and focuses on explaining the common variance, rather than the total variance, in the observed variables on the basis of a relatively few underlying factors.

Principal components is also similar to other multivariate procedures such as discriminant analysis and canonical correlation analysis in that they all involve linear combinations of correlated variables whose variable weights in the linear combination are derived on the basis of maximizing some statistical property. We have seen that principal components maximize the variance accounted for in the original variables. Linear discriminant function analysis, focusing on differences among groups, determines the weights for a linear composite that maximizes the between group relative to within group variance on that linear composite. Canonical correlation analysis, focusing on the relationships between two variable sets, derives a linear composite from each variable set such that the correlation between the two derived composites is maximized.

Principal components analysis is sometimes used prior to some factor analytic procedures to determine the dimensionality of the common factor space. It can also be used to select a subset of variables from a larger set of variables. That is, rather than substituting the principal components for the original variables we can select a set of variables that have high correlations with the principal components. Principal components analysis is also used in regression analysis to address multicollinearity problems (i.e., imprecise regression parameter estimates due to highly correlated independent variables). The technique is also useful in displaying multivariate data graphically so that, for example, outlying or atypical observations can be detected. This is based on the facts that the principal components represent the variation in the original variables and that there are considerably fewer graphical displays of the principal components to visually examine relative to the original variables. These and other applications of principal components analysis are subsequently discussed in this paper.

Principal components analysis searches for a few uncorrelated linear combinations of the original variables that capture most of the information in the original variables. We construct linear composites routinely, for example, test scores, quality of life indices, and so on. In most of these cases, each variable receives an equal weight in the linear composite. Indices force a p dimensional system into one dimension. For example, a set of p socioeconomic status (SES) indicators such as occupational level, educational level and income, which can be characterized as a p dimensional random vector $(x_1, x_2, \ldots, x_p)$, can be linearly transformed by $y = a_1x_1 + a_2x_2 + \ldots + a_px_p$ into a one dimensional SES index, y. In principal components analysis, the weights (i.e., $a_1, a_2, \ldots, a_p$) are mathematically determined to maximize the variation of the linear composite or, equivalently, to maximize the sum of the squared correlations of the principal component with the original variables. The linear composites (principal components) are ordered with respect to their variation so that the first few account for most of the variation present in the original variables, or equivalently, the first few principal components together have, overall, the highest possible squared multiple correlations with each of the original variables.

Geometrically, the first principal component is the line of closest fit to the n observations in the p dimensional variable space. It minimizes the sum of the squared distances of the n observation from the line in the variable space representing the first principal component. Distance is defined in a direction perpendicular to the line. The first two principal components define a plane of closest fit to the swarm of points in the p dimensional variable space. Equivalently, the second principal component is a line of closest fit to the residuals from the first principal component. The first three components define a three dimensional plane, called a hyperplane, of closest fit, and so on. If there are p variables, then there can be no more than p principal components. There can be fewer if there are linear dependencies among the variables. If all possible principal components are used, then they define a space which has the same dimension as the variable space and, hence, completely account for the variation in the variables. However, there is no advantage in retaining all of the principal components since we would have as many components as variables and, thus, would not have simplified matters.

Algebraically, the first principal component, y_1, is a linear combination of $x_1, x_2, \ldots, x_p$ (i.e., $y_1 = a_{11}x_1 + a_{12}x_2 + \ldots + a_{1p}x_p = \sum_{i=1}^{p} a_{1i}x_i$) such that the variance of y_1 is maximized given the constraint that the sum of the squared weights is equal to one (i.e., $\sum_{i=1}^{p} a_{1i}^2 = 1$). As we shall see, the random variables, x_i, can be either deviation from mean scores or standardized scores. If the variance of y_1 is maximized, then so is the sum of the squared correlations of y_1 with the original variables $x_1, x_2, \ldots, x_p$ (i.e., $\sum_{i=1}^{p} r_{y,x_i}^2$). Principal components analysis finds the optimal weight vector $(a_{11}, a_{12}, \ldots, a_{1p})$ and the associated variance of y_1 which is usually denoted by λ_1. The second principal component, y_2, involves finding a second weight vector $(a_{21}, a_{22}, \ldots, a_{2p})$ such that the variance of

$$y_2 = a_{21}x_1 + a_{22}x_2 + \ldots + a_{2p}x_p = \sum_{i=1}^{p} a_{2i}x_i$$

is maximized subject to the constraints that it is uncorrelated with the first principal component and $\sum_{i=1}^{p} a_{2i}^2 = 1$. This results in y_2 having the next largest sum of squared correlations with the original variables. However, the sum of squared correlations with the original variables, or equivalently, the variances of the principal components get smaller as successive principal components are extracted. The first two principal components together have the highest possible sum of squared multiple correlations (i.e., $\sum_{i=1}^{p} R_{x_i \cdot y_1, y_2}^2$) with the p variables.

This process can be continued until as many components as variables have been calculated. However, the first few principal components usually account for most of the variation in the variables and consequently our interest is focused on these, although, as we shall subsequently see, small components can also provide information about the structure of the data. The main statistics resulting from a principal components analysis are the variable weight vector $a = (a_1, a_2, \ldots, a_p)$ associated with each principal component and its associated variance, λ. As we shall see, the pattern of variable weights for a particular principal component are used to interpret the principal component and the magnitude of the variances of the principal components provide an indication of how well they account for the variability in the data. The relative sizes of the elements in a variable weight vector associated with a particular principal component indicate the relative contribution of the variable to the variance of the principal component, or, equivalently, the relative amounts of variation explained in the variables by the principal components. We will see that the correlations of the variables with a particular principal component are proportional to the elements of the associated weight vector. They can be obtained by multiplying all the elements in the weight vector by the square root of the variance ($\sqrt{\lambda}$) of the associated principal component.

Example

Let us apply the concepts that we have learned so far to a small correlation matrix involving five satisfaction variables generated from data collected from a large recent survey of U.S. armed forces personnel. The satisfaction variables analyzed here were part of a much larger set of satisfaction measures. They are satisfaction with job (SJ), satisfaction with job training (SJT), satisfaction with working conditions (SWC), satisfaction with medical care (SMC), and satisfaction with dental care (SDC). Each respondent was asked to rate their satisfaction on a 1 (very unsatisfactory) to 5 (very satisfactory) scale for each of these five aspects of the military. The correlation matrix among the five variables presented in Table 1.1 was generated for a large subsample of 9,147 married enlisted Army personnel. Note that all of the correlations are positive ranging from a low of .162 to a high of .620.

Since there are five variables, it is possible to extract five principal components from the correlation matrix under the reasonable assumption that for empirical data any one variable does not have a multiple correlation of 1 with the remaining four variables. The basic statistics of the principal components analysis are the five variances (latent roots) $\lambda_1, \ldots, \lambda_5$ ordered by size and the associated variable weight vectors (latent vectors) $a_1, \ldots, a_5$. The total variance in the system is five—the sum of the variances of the five standardized variables (i.e., $\sigma_i^2 = 1$ for $i = 1$ to 5). Each associated weight vector contains five elements, one corresponding to each variable. For example, $a_1 = [a_{11}, a_{12}, a_{13}, a_{14}, a_{15}]$ are the five weights associated with the largest principal component whose variance is λ_1. The latent roots and associated vectors are presented in Table 1.2.

TABLE 1.1

Correlations Among Five Satisfaction Variables for
Married Army Enlisted Personnel (N=9,147)

Variables	SJ	SJT	SWC	SMC	SDC
1) Satisfaction with Job (SJ)	1.000	.451	.511	.197	.162
2) Satisfaction with Job Training (SJT)		1.000	.445	.252	.238
3) Satisfaction with Working Conditions (SWC)			1.000	.301	.227
4) Satisfaction with Medical Care (SMC)				1.000	.620
5) Satisfaction with DentalCare (SDC)					1.000

TABLE 1.2

Latent Roots (Variances) and Latent Vectors of
Correlation Matrix of Satisfaction Variables

Variable	Latent Vector				
	a_1	a_2	a_3	a_4	a_5
SJ	.442	.443	.301	−.716	.074
SJT	.457	.290	−.832	.114	.034
SWC	.479	.308	.454	.658	−.185
SMC	.443	−.531	.095	.060	.714
SDC	.412	−.586	.032	−.191	−.670
λ_i	2.370	1.202	.573	.484	.373

The sum of squares of the five elements in each of these five columns add up to 1. The sum of the cross products of any two columns
add up to 0. The elements in the first column are the weights associated with the linear composite that has maximum variance or, equivalently, has the largest sum of the squared correlations with the five
variables. The linear composite is .442 SJ + .457 SJT + .479 SWC +
.443 SMC + .412 SDC. The weights are about equal so that each satisfaction variable is about equally represented in the linear composite.
Accordingly, the first principal component could be interpreted as a
measure of general satisfaction. The variance of the first principal
component is 2.370. It explains (100 · 2.370/5) or 47.4% of the total
variance of the five variables. The second principal component is the
linear composite .443 SJ + .290 SJT + .308 SWC − .531 SMC −
.586 SDC. Since the first three weights are associated with job related
satisfaction variables and are positive and the last two weights are associated with health care satisfaction variables and are negative, the

14

TABLE 1.3
Principal Component Loading Matrix for Satisfaction Variables

| Variable | Principal Component | | | | |
	1	2	3	4	5
SJ	.680	.485	.228	−.498	.045
SJT	.704	.318	−.630	.079	.021
SWC	.738	.338	.344	.458	−.113
SMC	.682	−.582	.072	.042	.436
SDC	.634	−.642	−.024	−.133	−.409

second principal component is interpreted as a contrast between job
satisfaction and health satisfaction. High scores on this component
are associated with higher scores on the three job satisfaction variables and low scores on the two health care satisfaction variables. The
second principal component has a variance of 1.202 and accounts for
(100 · 1.202/5) or 24.0% of the total variance of the five variables.
Together the first two components account for 47.4% + 24.0% or
71.4% of the variance in the five variables. Since the first principal
component has all positive weights, the second and subsequent principal components must have a pattern of positive and negative weights
since the cross products between any two columns must disappear.
The remaining three smaller components will not be interpreted because, as we shall see, they are not important enough by most criteria.
Thus, we have reduced the dimensionality of our observations from
five to two.

The loadings (correlations) of the variables with the five principal
components are presented in Table 1.3. The elements (correlations) in
each column are proportional to the corresponding column elements
(latent vector) in Table 1.2. The sum of the squared correlations for
each column equal the associated latent root, the amount of variance
explained. The information presented in each of Tables 1.2 and 1.3 is
equivalent, but many researchers prefer to interpret the pattern of correlations rather than the proportional elements in the associated latent
vector. The preference for correlations probably stems from the factor
analytic tradition of interpreting factor loading matrices which will be
discussed subsequently. Also, the size of the correlations for a particular principal component directly reflects the importance of the components in explaining variation in the original variables.

2. BASIC CONCEPTS OF PRINCIPAL COMPONENTS ANALYSIS

The variance of a linear composite

$$\sum_{i=1}^{p} a_i x_i \text{ is } \sum_{i=1}^{p} \sum_{j=1}^{p} a_i a_j \sigma_{ij}$$

where σ_{ij} is the covariance between the ith and jth variables. This is a straightforward generalization of the variance of a linear composite of two variables, $y = a_1 x_1 + a_2 x_2$ which is $a_1^2 \sigma_1^2 + a_2^2 \sigma_2^2 + 2a_1 a_2 \sigma_{12}$. The variance of a linear composite can also be more easily expressed in matrix algebra as $a'Ca$ where a is the vector of variable weights and C is the covariance matrix. Principal components analysis finds the weight vector a that maximizes $a'Ca$ given the constraint that

$$\sum_{i=1}^{p} a_i^2 = a'a = 1.$$

The size of the elements of a must be constrained or otherwise we could arbitrarily make the variance of the linear composite large by selecting large weights.

A linear composite can be based on a covariance matrix, as above, or a correlation matrix, R, which is a covariance matrix of standardized variables. Similarly, principal components analysis can be based on either a covariance matrix, C, or correlation matrix, R.

In many cases the units in which the variables are measured are arbitrary. This is particularly true in the behavioral and social sciences where many variables are scales. Even if the variables are measured in the same units, the variances of the variables may differ considerably. For example, anthropomorphic body measurements in centimeters would show a large variation in body height and a relatively small variation in wrist circumference for a sample of adult males. We shall see later that principal components analysis of covariance matrices with large differences in variances among the variables causes problems. The major problem is that variables with large variances automatically get large weights in the principal component and variables with small variances automatically get negligible weights. This is because the way to maximize the variance of a linear composite is to give large weights to the variables with large variances. Most of our discussion and examples will focus on correlation matrices.

If there are no exact linear dependencies among the p variables, then there are as many principal components as variables. A linear dependency means that any one variable in the variable set can be written as an exact linear combination of one or more of the remaining variables. An example of a linear dependency in a set of three variables is $x_1 = \beta_1 x_2 + \beta_2 x_3$. Since there is no error term in the relationship, this is equivalent to a multiple correlation of one between the dependent variable x_1, and the independent variables x_2 and x_3. Exact nonlinear dependencies among the variables such as $x_1 = \beta_1 x_2^2 + \beta_2 x_2 x_3$ have no impact on the dimensionality of a linear space or, consequently, the number of principal components. If there are exact linear dependencies, then the variables are redundant since one or more variables can be dropped from the variable set without any loss of information. We can perfectly predict the values of the excluded variables from the remaining variables. When we have exact linear dependencies, then the dimensionality of the variable space is accordingly reduced. The number of principal components is equal to the dimensionality of the variable space. In most cases, the dimensionality of the variable space is equal to the number of variables since we rarely encounter exact linear dependencies in real empirical data sets. The goal of principal components is to find p linear transformations of the p variables, the principal components.

If we have a set of n observations (e.g., individuals), on p variables, then we can find the largest principal component of R, the correlation matrix, as the weight vector $[a_{11}, a_{12}, a_{13}, \ldots, a_{1p}]$ which maximizes the variance of

$$\sum_{i=1}^{p} a_{1i} x_i \text{ given that } \sum_{i=1}^{p} a_{1i}^2 = 1.$$

In this case, the x_i are standardized variables. We can then define the second largest principal component of R as the weight vector, $[a_{21}, a_{22}, a_{23}, \ldots, a_{2p}]$ which maximizes the variance of

$$\sum_{i=1}^{p} a_{2i} x_i \text{ given that } \sum_{i=1}^{p} a_{2i}^2 = 1$$

and that principal component 2 is linearly independent of principal component 1. The independence condition is specified by the constraint that

$$\sum_{i=1}^{p} a_{1i} a_{2i} = 0.$$

Continuing, we can define a third largest principal component as the weight vector $[a_{31}, a_{32}, a_{33}, \ldots, a_{3p}]$ which maximizes the variance of

$$\sum_{i=1}^{p} a_{3i}x_i \text{ given that } \sum_{i=1}^{p} a_{3i}^2 = 1$$

and that the third principal component, $[a_{31}, a_{32}, \ldots, a_{3p}]$ is orthogonal (i.e., independent) to the first two principal components. These two orthogonality conditions are

$$\sum_{i=1}^{p} a_{3i}a_{1i} = \sum_{i=1}^{p} a_{3i}a_{2i} = 0.$$

We can continue this scenario down to the last or pth principal component.

The sum of the variances of the principal components is equal to the sum of the variances of the original variables. That is

$$\sum_{i=1}^{p} \lambda_i = \sum_{i=1}^{p} \sigma_i^2.$$

where λ_i is the variance of the ith principal component. If the variables are standardized, then

$$\sum_{i=1}^{p} \lambda_i = p.$$

The proportion of variance in the original p variables that k principal components accounts for can be easily calculated as

$$\sum_{i=1}^{k} \lambda_i / p$$

where k is less than p. The proportion of variance that any single principal component accounts for is simply λ_i / p. If the sum of the variances of the first few principal components is close to p, the number of original variables, then we have captured most of the information in the original variables by a few principal components which are linear transformations of the original variables.

It can be shown that the above definition of principal components leads to the matrix equation $Ra = \lambda a$ where λ is the latent root of the correlation matrix R and a is its associated latent vector. Latent roots are sometimes called eigenvalues and latent vectors are sometimes called eigenvectors. They are also called characteristic roots and vectors, respectively. This matrix equation can be solved for λ and a, the basic statistics of principal components analysis. If the matrix R is nonsingular (i.e., no exact linear dependencies among the variables exist), then there are p latent roots, λ_i, and p associated latent vectors a_i, that satisfy the equation. It can be shown that the largest latent root (λ_1) of R is the variance of the first or largest principal component of R and its associated vector

$$a_1 = \begin{bmatrix} a_{11} \\ a_{12} \\ \cdot \\ \cdot \\ \cdot \\ a_{1p} \end{bmatrix}$$

is the set of weights for the first principal component that maximize the variance of

$$\sum_{i=1}^{p} a_{1i} x_i.$$

The second largest latent root of R is the variance of the second largest principal component and its associated vector

$$a_2 = \begin{bmatrix} a_{21} \\ a_{22} \\ \cdot \\ \cdot \\ \cdot \\ a_{2p} \end{bmatrix}$$

is the set of weights for the second principal component that results in the linear composite or principal component with the next largest variance. The pth or last latent root (λ_p) is the variance of the last or smallest principal component and its associated vector

$$a_p = \begin{bmatrix} a_{p1} \\ a_{p2} \\ \cdot \\ \cdot \\ \cdot \\ a_{pp} \end{bmatrix}$$

are the variable weights defining the smallest principal component. If the latent roots are all distinct, then there are p distinct associated latent vectors. This is typically the case for sample correlation and covariance matrices. We will subsequently discuss the case in which some of the latent roots of a correlation or covariance matrix are equal.

Since the principal components are uncorrelated, each one makes an independent contribution to accounting for the variance of the original variables. If, for example, x_i correlates r_{i1} with the largest/first principal component and r_{i2} with the second largest principal component, then, since the two principal components are uncorrelated, the squared multiple correlation of x_i with the first two principal components is $r_{i1}^2 + r_{i2}^2$. The first k largest principal components maximize the sum of these squared multiple correlations across all the variables. This is a generalization of the fact that the first principal component maximizes the sum of the squared simple correlations of the variables with the largest principal component.

Hence, there are p linear transformations (principal components) of the original p variables. They are

$$y_1 = \sum_{j=1}^{p} a_{1j} x_j$$

$$y_2 = \sum_{j=1}^{p} a_{2j} x_j$$

.
.
.

$$y_p = \sum_{j=1}^{p} a_{pj} x_j.$$

They can be expressed more succinctly in matrix algebra as

$$y = A'x$$

where y is a p element vector of principal component scores, A' is a $p \times p$ matrix of latent vectors with the ith row corresponding to the elements of the latent vector associated with the ith latent root, and x is a p element column vector of the original variables. This is a linear transformation of a p element random vector x into a p element random vector y, the principal components.

From the definition of principal components, we have $A'A=I$. Note that A is the matrix with latent vectors as columns, A' is the transpose of A with latent vectors as rows, and I is the $p \times p$ identity matrix with ones in the principal diagonal and zeros elsewhere. $A'A=I$ simply indicates that the cross products of any two latent vectors are 0 and the sum of squares of the elements for a given latent vector are equal to 1.

For example, since $A'A=I$, the element in the 3rd row and 3rd column of I is a 1 (since it is on the principal diagonal of I) and is obtained by multiplying the 3rd row of A' by the 3rd column of A element by element and summing the cross products. That is,

$$\sum_{i=1}^{p} a_{3i}\, a_{3i} = \sum_{i=1}^{p} a_{3i}^2 = 1$$

or in matrix terminology $a_3'a_3 = 1$. The element in the 3rd row and 4th column of I is 0 (since it is an off-diagonal element of I) and is obtained by multiplying the 3rd row of A' by the 4th column of A element by element and summing the products. That is,

$$\sum_{i=1}^{p} a_{4i}\, a_{3i} = 0 \text{ or } a_4'a_3 = 0$$

since the latent vectors are orthogonal or perpendicular to one another. Each element of I is the result of the multiplying a row vector from A' by a column vector from A. This is, in fact, the definition of matrix multiplication.

Since the ith latent root and its associated latent root must satisfy the matrix equation $Ra_i = \lambda_i a_i$, we have, premultiplying by a_i', $a_i' Ra_i = \lambda_i a_i'a_i = \lambda_i$ for the variance of the ith principal component since

$$a_i'a_i = \sum_{j=1}^{p} a_{ij}^2 = 1.$$

We can succinctly express the facts that $Ra_1 = \lambda_1 a_1$, $Ra_2 = \lambda_2 a_2$, . . . , $Ra_p = \lambda_p a_p$ by combining these relations in one matrix expression as $RA = A\Lambda$ where A is a matrix of eigenvectors as column vectors, and Λ is a diagonal matrix of the corresponding latent roots ordered from largest to smallest.

The elements of Λ, the diagonal matrix of latent roots, have to be in the same order as their associated latent vectors, the columns of A, in order for the matrix equation $RA = A\Lambda$ to hold. That is, the latent root in the ith row and column of Λ must have its corresponding latent vector in the ith column of A. We can use any arbitrary ordering of the latent roots in Λ as long as we use the same ordering of the associated latent roots in A, but it makes more sense to order them with respect to their importance.

We can generalize from $a_i'Ra_i = \lambda_i$ as the equation for the variance of the *ith* principal component using matrix algebra to obtain the covariance matrix of the principal components as $A'RA = \Lambda$ where A' is the transpose of A (i.e., rows are eigenvectors). That is, since $RA = A\Lambda$, we can premultiply both sides of this expression to obtain $A'RA = A'A\Lambda = \Lambda$ since $A'A = I$. Also, since $RA = A\Lambda$, we can post multiply both sides of this matrix expression by A' to get $RAA' = A\Lambda A'$. Since $AA' = I$, $R = A\Lambda A'$. Thus, we can decompose R into a product of three matrices involving latent vectors and latent roots. The goal of principal components analysis is to decompose the correlation matrix. That is, explain the variation expressed in R in terms of weighting vectors (latent vectors) of the principal components and variances (latent roots) of the principal components. The decomposition of R is a key concept in principal components analysis and we shall discuss it further in a subsequent section.

Many times it is easier to interpret the principal component when the elements of the latent vector are transformed to correlations of the variables with the particular principal components. This can be done by multiplying each of the elements of a particular latent vector, a_i, by the square root of the associated latent root, $\sqrt{\lambda_i}$. Thus the correlations of the variables with the *ith* principal component is $\sqrt{\lambda_i}a_i$. The correlations of the variables with the principal components are sometimes called loadings, a term borrowed from factor analysis. Variables that correlate highly with a particular principal component give meaning to that component.

Like any other statistical inference problem, we can talk about population parameters associated with the principal components and the sample estimates of them. For example, there are population latent roots and associated latent vectors and sample estimates of them. Procedures have been established for estimating standard errors for these parameters, but the procedures are based primarily on covariance matrices and assume multivariate normality. Inference procedures based on correlation matrices are much more troublesome and consequently not much has been developed in this area. In addition, we use principal components primarily as a tool to describe a sample of observations. We are not interested in testing specific hypotheses, except for possibly the hypothesis that the last latent roots are equal, i.e., $\lambda_k = \lambda_{k+1} = \ldots = \lambda_p$. This test could help us decide how many principal components to retain since, if the last k latent roots are equal, then the latent vectors associated with them are arbitrary, as we shall see, and, hence, should be discarded. For a discussion of statistical inference in principal components analysis the interested reader is referred to Anderson (1963), Lawley (1963), and Morrison (1976).

How many and which principal components to retain depend, in part, on the goals of the analysis. If we simply want to describe a variable set without regard to subsequent uses, then retaining the k largest principal components might be adequate. If we want to use the principal components as predictors of a dependent variable, then we should consider their correlations with the dependent variable as well. Presently, we will be concerned with simply describing a data set by principal components without regard to their subsequent uses as independent variables in a regression analysis or as substitutes for the original variables in multivariate procedures such as discriminant analysis and canonical correlation analysis. The role of principal components analysis in these other analyses will be discussed in the following chapters.

We will now discuss some "rules of thumb" or criteria designed to help us decide on how many principal components to retain. Kaiser (1960) recommends dropping those principal components of a correlation matrix with latent roots less than one. He argues that principal components with variances less than one contain less information than a single standardized variable whose variance is one. In addition, his rule was developed with reference to factor analysis rather than to principal components analysis. Holding rigidly to Kaiser's criteria may result in discarding principal components that, while small, may be important. For example, some variables may not be very well represented by the larger principal components and we may want to retain smaller principal components that better represent those variables.

Jolliffe (1972) has suggested that Kaiser's rule tends to throw away too much information and on the basis of simulation studies has suggested a cutoff of .7 for correlation matrices. Part of his argument is based on the fact that a population latent root ≥ 1 can result in a corresponding sample latent root considerably less than 1 because of sampling error. This rule can be extended to covariance matrices by using the cutoff $.7\bar{\lambda}$ where $\bar{\lambda}$ is the average size of the latent roots of the covariance matrix.

Cattell (1966) proposes the use of a "scree" graph to help decide on how many principal components to retain. The scree graph involves plotting the latent roots and finding a point where the line joining the points is steep to the left of the point k, and not steep to the right of k. One then retains k principal components. The problem with this method is that steep and non-steep are arbitrary and that for many principal component analyses no such lines are evident.

Another criteria is to retain enough principal components to account for a given percentage of variation, e.g., 80%. All of these rules are arbitrary and should be applied with caution. For example, Jolliffe's criterion of $\lambda = .7$ can, in certain instances, result in retaining twice as many components as Kaiser's criterion of $\lambda = 1$. The more principal components relative to the number of variables that are retained, the less parsimonious our description of the data. In addition, smaller principal components are, in general, harder to interpret than larger ones.

3. GEOMETRICAL
PROPERTIES OF PRINCIPAL COMPONENTS

For a three dimensional random variable characterized by a vector (x_1, x_2, x_3), we can actually plot the observations as points in ordinary three dimensional space. For example, the random vector (5, 4, 8) can be represented as a value of 5 with respect to the x_1 axis, 4 with respect to the x_2 axis, and 8 with respect to the x_3 axis. The x_1, x_2, and x_3 coordinate axes are mutually perpendicular. The coordinates of a point tell us the location of a point in space with respect to the particular set of coordinate axes. If we plot a data set of three dimensional observations, then under certain conditions (e.g., multivariate normality) they will form an egg shaped swarm of points. A line is a one dimensional subspace in this ordinary three dimensional space. A plane is a two dimensional subspace. Sometimes a line or a plane can be found that will lie close to most of the points and then the three dimensional swarm of points can be essentially characterized by a one or two dimensional subspace. This one or two dimensional subspace captures most of the variation (i.e., the distances between observations) in the original three dimensional space.

We can generalize these ideas to higher dimensional spaces where we can no longer plot and visualize the swarm of points. A random vector of 10 variables $(x_1, x_2, . . , x_{10})$ can be considered as a point in ten dimensional space where a particular observation, say, (4, 10, . . . , 3) represents the values on the $x_1, x_2, . . , x_{10}$ coordinate axes. The coordinates locate the points in the ten dimensional space. In this case, principal component analysis finds a lower dimensional space of say, three dimensions, that provides the best fit to the 10 dimensional swarm of points. We can then represent the points with respect to the coordinate axes, the principal components, defining this subspace. For example, if the best fitting subspace is three dimensional, then three coordinate axes are needed to represent it. An observation can now be represented by its three coordinates on the three new coordinate axes (y_1, y_2, y_3) as contrasted to being represented by the 10 coordinate axes $(x_1, x_2, \ldots, x_{10})$ of the original variables. The idea is to use the first k principal components which are the coordinate axes or basis for a k dimensional subspace of the p dimensional variable space in which most of the variation in the p variables is contained.

The geometrical properties of principal components can be elucidated by some two dimensional figures. Let us assume that we have a sample of observations on two standardized variables, x_1 and x_2. We can use x_1 and x_2 as coordinate axes and plot the standardized scores as in Figure 3.1.

From the shape of the scatterplot we can see that there is a substantial correlation between x_1 and x_2, perhaps a correlation of about .90. There are two variables, and if the variables are not perfectly correlated, two principal components are required to completely account for the variation in the two variables. The first principal component is a new coordinate axis in the variable space which is oriented in a direction that maximizes the variation of the projections of the points on the new coordinate axis, the first principal component. The projection of a point on a coordinate axis is the numerical value on the coordinate axis at which a line from the point drawn perpendicular to the axis intersects the axis. Note that the swarm of points has an elliptical shape and that the first principal component is the principal axis of this ellipse. It turns out that for two standardized variables, the first principal component always forms a 45 degree angle with x_1 and hence x_2 (i.e., it bisects the angle $x_1 0 x_2$) irrespective of the size of the correlation as long as the correlation is not zero. The latent vector associated the largest latent root of the two by two correlation matrix is always

$$a_1 = \begin{bmatrix} .71 \\ .71 \end{bmatrix}.$$

The direction cosine is the cosine of the angle that the principal component coordinate axis makes with a particular variable coordinate axis. It follows that there are as many direction cosines for a particular principal component as there are variables or, equivalently, the number of elements in each latent vector. In fact, the elements of the latent vector are the direction cosines of the first principal component with the x_1 and x_2 axes, respectively. The largest principal component makes an angle of 45 degrees with both x_1 and x_2 and the cosine of 45

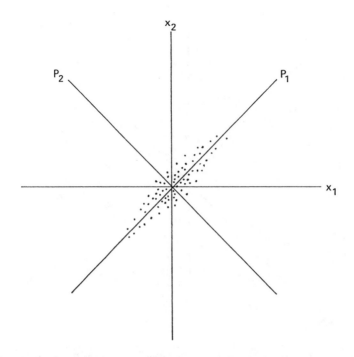

Figure 3.1: Scatterplot of Two Standardized Variables

degrees is .71. As discussed previously, the length of each latent vector is 1 and if we perpendicularly project this unit length vector on both x_1 and x_2, the respective projections are each equal to .71. Thus, the projections of the unit length latent vector variable representing a particular principal component, on each of the variables coordinate axes are equal to the direction cosines. This is illustrated in Figure 3.2. Harman (1976) gives a good discussion of the basic trigonometric and geometric concepts associated with principal components analysis.

For three or more variables, the elements of the latent vector for the largest principal component usually differ from one another. They are only exactly equal if all of the correlations in the correlation matrix are exactly equal. Correlation matrices, especially large ones, rarely have all correlations equal to one another. However, as we shall see later, if the correlations are fairly similar in magnitude, then the elements of the latent vector for the largest principal component will also be similar in magnitude. These elements of the latent vector, the direction cosines, are the directions of the principal component axis

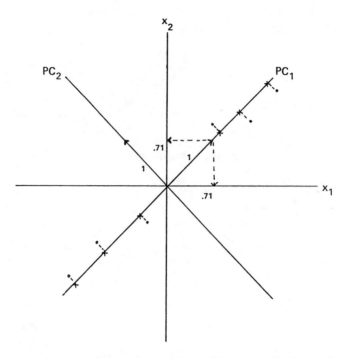

Figure 3.2: One Dimensional Representation by Largest Principal Components of Two Dimensional Data

with respect to each of the variables. For example, in the case of three or more variables, a direction cosine close to one (element of the latent vector) for a particular variable indicates that the direction of the principal component is close to the direction of that variable in the p dimensional space.

If the correlation between the two variables is high, then most of the information contained in the two dimensional swarm of observation can be represented by their projection onto the single largest principal component. This is true for Figure 3.1 and illustrated in more detail with a few observations in Figure 3.2.

There are six observations in Figure 3.2 representing an almost perfect correlation between x_1 and x_2. The perpendicular projections of these six points onto the largest principal component axis are indicated by the dotted lines. These projections are the principal component scores of the linear transformation $y_1 = .71x_1 + .71x_2$. Note that for this pattern of projections, the principal component scores for the largest principal component contains about as much information with regard to the scatter of the observation as the two dimensional scatter in the space of the original two variables, x_1 and x_2. That is because the observations essentially fall on a straight line, the largest principal component. We have captured the information concerning the scatter in a two dimensional space by projecting the points onto a one dimensional subspace, the largest principal component. Another property of the first principal component, evident from Figure 3.2, is that it minimizes the sum of the squared distances of the observations from their perpendicular projections onto the largest principal component. For this reason, the first principal component is sometimes referred to as the line of closest fit.

Since the second principal component is orthogonal, or perpendicular, to the first principal component (i.e., they intersect at a right angle), the vector product $a'_1 a_2$ where

$$a_1 = \begin{bmatrix} .71 \\ .71 \end{bmatrix},$$

the latent vector associated with the largest principal component and

$$a_2 = \begin{bmatrix} a_{21} \\ a_{22} \end{bmatrix}$$

the latent vector associated with the second principal component, must equal 0 by definition. That is, two vectors a and b emanating from the origin at right angles to each other have the property that $a'b = b'a = 0$. Thus,

$$[.71 \ .71] \begin{bmatrix} a_{21} \\ a_{22} \end{bmatrix} = .71 a_{21} + .71 a_{22} = 0.$$

With the constraint that $a_{21}^2 + a_{22}^2 = 1$, it can be shown that $a_{21} = .71$ and $a_{22} = .71$. Thus $a_2 = \begin{bmatrix} -.71 \\ .71 \end{bmatrix}$. The unit vector representing the direction of the second principal component is also shown in Figure 3.2.

The direction cosines of the second principal component are the projections of this unit length vector on the x_1 and x_2 axes, respectively. That is, if we drop a perpendicular line from the tip of the arrow onto the x_1 axis, we find $-.71$ as the value of the projection. The perpendicular projection on x_2 is .71. Note that the variation of points in the direction of the second principal component is considerably smaller than the variation of the points in the direction of the largest principal component. That is, if we project the points perpendicularly onto the second principal component, these are the second principal component scores and their variation on this line is considerably smaller than the variation of the projections onto the first principal component. The perpendicular projections of the six points onto the second principal component would result in principal component scores with virtually no variation when compared to the variation of the projections of these six points on the largest principal component.

Note that the two orthogonal principal components function as just another frame of reference or set of coordinate axes to represent the swarm of observations in the two dimensional variable space. The projections of the observations on the two principal components contain the exact same amount of information as the projections of the observations on the two original variables. For example, distances between points in the two dimensional swarm are the same using either set of coordinate axes. However, if we use as many principal components as variables to represent the swarm of points or observations, then we have not simplified the data because we have not reduced the dimensionality of the data set. The object of principal components analysis is to represent a p dimensional space by a considerably lower dimensional subspace that represents most of the variation in the original p dimensional space. The information is contained in the projections of the p dimensional points onto the k dimensional subspace where k is much smaller than p.

If the two variables are highly correlated as in Figures 3.1 and 3.2, then the two dimensional variable space can be adequately represented by a one dimensional subspace, the first principal component. For example, if x_1 and x_2 had a correlation of .90, then the first principal component $y_1 = .71 x_1 + .71 x_2$ would have a variance equal to $(.71)^2 + (.71)^2 + 2(.71)^2(.90) = 1.90$. Since the variance of each of the two standardized variables is 1, the total variance in the two variable system is 2. The largest principal component has a variance equal to 1.90 so it accounts for a proportion of (1.90/2) or .95 of the variation in the two variables, x_1 and x_2. As we discussed earlier, this turns out to be the largest eigenvalue of the correlation matrix. We can see this by solving the matrix equation $Ra = \lambda a$. For our two variable example,

$$R = \begin{bmatrix} 1 & .90 \\ .90 & 1 \end{bmatrix} \text{ and } a = \begin{bmatrix} .71 \\ .71 \end{bmatrix}$$

so that

$$\begin{bmatrix} 1 & .90 \\ .90 & 1 \end{bmatrix} \begin{bmatrix} .71 \\ .71 \end{bmatrix} = \lambda \begin{bmatrix} .71 \\ .71 \end{bmatrix}$$

Postmultiplying the first row of R, [1 .90], by $\begin{bmatrix} .71 \\ .71 \end{bmatrix}$ we have $1(.71)$ $+ .90(.71) = 1.349$. Equating the first element on both sides of the matrix equation we have $1.349 = \lambda\ .71$ or $\lambda = 1.9$.

As discussed previously, the latent vectors for the first and second principal components are $\begin{bmatrix} .71 \\ .71 \end{bmatrix}$ and $\begin{bmatrix} -.71 \\ .71 \end{bmatrix}$, respectively, regardless of the magnitude of the correlation. The amount of variation for the original variables, however, explained by each principal component differs depending on the degree of correlation. In the case of a perfect correlation $R = \begin{bmatrix} 1 & 1 \\ 1 & 1 \end{bmatrix}$ and using the relation $Ra = \lambda a$, we have

$$\begin{bmatrix} 1 & 1 \\ 1 & 1 \end{bmatrix} \begin{bmatrix} .71 \\ .71 \end{bmatrix} = \lambda \begin{bmatrix} .71 \\ .71 \end{bmatrix}.$$

Equating the first element on both sides of the equation, we have $1(.71) + 1(.71) = \lambda(.71)$ or $\lambda = 2$. Thus, the variance of the larger principal component is 2. The total variance in the two standardized variables is 2 so that the first principal component explains 100% (2/2) of the variation in the two standardized variables, x_1 and x_2. Knowing that the latent vector or direction cosines associated with the second principal component is $\begin{bmatrix} -.71 \\ .71 \end{bmatrix}$, we can solve for the associated second largest latent root. Using the matrix equation as before, we find $1(-.71) + 1(.71) = \lambda\ (.71)$ or $\lambda = 0$. So the second latent root is zero and the variation in x_1 and x_2 explained by the second principal component is zero. This seems reasonable since we already know that the first principal component explained 100% of the variation in x_1, and x_2. Since the value of the second principal component is a constant of zero for all observations, $0 = -.71\ x_1 + .71\ x_2$ or $x_1 = x_2$. This indicates that x_1 is a perfect linear function of x_2. It tells us that x_1 is perfectly correlated with x_2. So latent vectors associated with zero latent roots indicate dependencies among variables. We shall say more about this later.

Even though the latent root associated with the second principal component is zero, it still has a unique direction given by its associated latent vector, $a_2 = \begin{bmatrix} -.71 \\ .71 \end{bmatrix}$. That is, it has to be perpendicular to the first principal component even if it turns out that all of the observations have a zero projection on it.

Returning to our example with a correlation of .90, we showed that the variance of the first principal component was 1.9. Since the total variability in the system of two standardized variables is 2, we may surmise that the variance of the second principal component is .1. We can verify this by substituting into the principal components equation $Ra = \lambda a$. Substituting we have

$$\begin{bmatrix} 1 & .90 \\ .90 & 1 \end{bmatrix} \begin{bmatrix} -.71 \\ .71 \end{bmatrix} = \lambda \begin{bmatrix} -.71 \\ .71 \end{bmatrix}$$

which gives $\lambda = .1$.

If the two variables have a zero correlation, then the swarm of observations in the variable space typically has a circular appearance as shown in Figure 3.3.

Looking at the circular swarm of points in Figure 3.3, we can see that there is no coordinate axis that maximizes the variance of the projections upon it. That is, there is no unique direction in which we can place a coordinate axis that maximizes variation. One direction is as good as another. So the direction cosines, or elements of the latent vector associated with the largest latent root are not unique. There are an infinite number of directions represented by the latent vector for the largest principal component. Intuitively, we can see that no matter where we place the coordinate axis, the variance of the projections of the points on this axis is always the same since the spread of the points on each possible coordinate axis is equal to the diameter of the circle representing the swarm of points. A few directions are illustrated in Figure 3.3. Each explains the same amount of variance as each of the original variables which is one.

Regression analysis for the two variable cases also results in a line of closest fit. However, the regression line is determined by minimizing the sum of squared distances of the points from the line in the direction of the dependent variable. These distances are not perpendicular to the line as they are in principal components analysis. The differences between the principal component line of best fit and the regression line of best fit is illustrated in Figure 3.4.

When one standardized variable is regressed on another, there can be an infinite number of regression lines, each with a different slope, depending upon the degree of correlation. However, there is only one unique principal component line regardless of the magnitude of correlation for the case of two standardized variables.

Before we leave the two dimensional case, we will briefly return to the problem of conducting a principal components analysis on a covariance matrix from a geometrical perspective. If the variance of one variable is a large multiple of the other variables, then the direction cosine for that variable will be close to 1 and the direction cosines associated with the remaining variables will be close to zero. In other words, the principal component is oriented in the direction of the

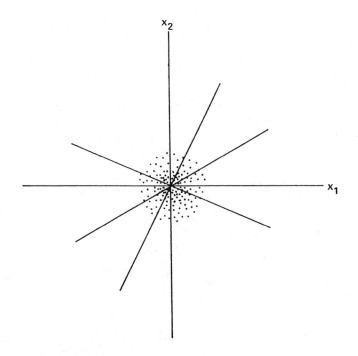

Figure 3.3: Distribution of Two Uncorrelated Variables

variable with the largest variance. This is the direction that maximizes the variation of the largest principal component as illustrated in Figure 3.5.

From Figure 3.5 we can see that the variance of x_1 is high compared to x_2. The largest principal component therefore, has a large direction cosine for x_1 and a small one for x_2 as illustrated in Figure 3.5. It can maximize its variation by orienting itself in the direction of x_1. In a case like this where we have such extreme differences in variances, we could use the variable with the largest variances as a good approximation for the first principal component. Not much is gained by doing a principal component analysis in this situation. We would be better off standardizing the variables so that a single variable would not dominate the analysis. The orientation of the swarm of observations, an approximate ellipse, for a given correlation, and hence the direction of the first principal component, depends on the scales of the variables. It turns out that the solution of a principal component analysis is not invariant with respect to changes in the scales of the variables. Not invariant means that the principal components of

32

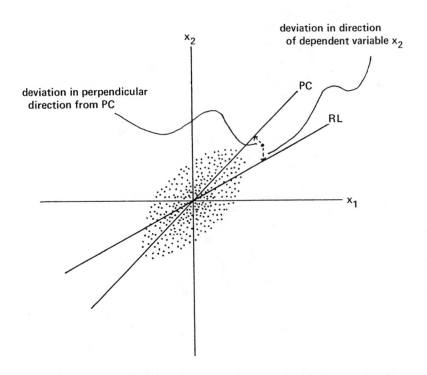

Figure 3.4 Principal Component and Regression Line

the covariance matrix have no direct relationship with those of the corresponding correlation matrix. That is, the latent roots and associated latent vectors of a covariance matrix cannot be algebraically transformed into the latent roots and associated latent vectors of the corresponding correlation matrix.

Let us now move from the two dimensional model to a three dimensional model. While no diagrams or figures will be presented, we can still visualize patterns of swarms of observations in three dimensional space. Again, for convenience, we assume that all variables are standardized. If the three variables are uncorrelated, then the swarm of points in the three dimensional space will take the form of a sphere, or ball, with the density of points greatest near the origin and decreasing towards the surface of the sphere. Like the circular density in two dimensional space, there is no unique direction for a coordinate axis that maximizes the variation of the points projected onto it. Every direction has a variance of 1, the same as the original observations. There is no way to simplify the structure of the observations.

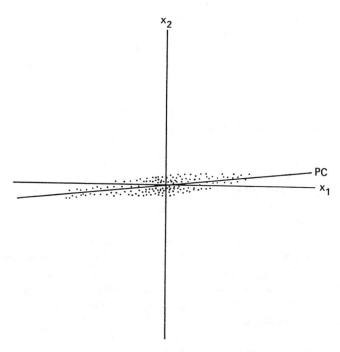

Figure 3.5: Largest Principal Component of Covariance Matrix

We might as well use the original uncorrelated variables. It turns out that all three latent roots are equal to 1, so there is no dominant latent root that would have a unique vector associated with it.

For moderate size correlations among the three variables, the swarm of points would take the shape of an egg or an ellipsoid. The largest principal component would take the direction of the principal axis of the ellipsoid. The second largest principal component would be orthogonal to the first principal component but in a direction that would maximize the variance of the projections of the points on this second coordinate axis. The third largest or smallest principal component would be orthogonal to the first two principal components and, hence, perpendicular to the plane defined by the first two principal components.

If the variables are highly correlated, the swarm of points will have more of a cigar shaped pattern with one large principal component going through the center of the cigar in the direction which the cigar is pointed. The second and third principal components will be orthogonal to the first and be considerably smaller. The second principal component would be orthogonal to the axis of the cigar and be in the direction that maximizes variation. For example, if the cross section of the cigar is elliptically shaped, then the second principal component would be in the direction of the principal axis of that ellipse. The third principal component would be orthogonal to the plane defined by the first two principal components.

If the three variables are perfectly correlated $(r = 1)$, then the swarm of points will fall exactly on a straight line. A single principal component captures all of the variation in the original three variables. Since the three variables each have unit variance, and the first principal component accounts for all of this variance, the first principal component has a variance of three. Thus, the largest latent root is three, and the remaining two latent roots are each equal to zero since there is no variation in the points in any direction orthogonal to the largest principal component. The latent vectors associated with the two zero latent roots are not unique since there are no directions in which variance can be maximized. It is zero no matter which direction we go. If the last two principal components are equal, then the variation orthogonal to the first principal component is circular and there is no unique direction for the latent vectors associated with the two equal latent roots.

It very seldom occurs in practice that one or more of the latent roots are exactly equal to zero or two or more of the latent roots are exactly equal to each other. However, there are occasions when one or more of the latent roots are close to zero or two or more of the latent roots are very close to one another in magnitude. In this instance, the resulting latent vectors for a sample correlation matrix could be very unstable.

There are a number of computer algorithms for computing principal components. A detailed discussion of one, the power method, is presented by Dunteman (1984b). Jolliffe (1986) describes the major algorithms and the computer packages in which they are embedded. All of the major computer packages such as SAS and SPSS provide routines for principal components analysis. The outputs for the different programs are quite similar. For example, SAS output includes the following: means and standard deviations of the variables; the variable correlation matrix; the complete set of latent roots and their associated latent vectors; a listing of the principal components scores; and graphical plots of scores for pairs of principal components. SAS also provides for the rotation of the k largest components retained on the basis of various criteria (e.g., $\lambda \geq 1$) or specified a priori by the user. Both the original principal component scores or the rotated component scores can be saved in specified files for use in subsequent analyses.

Example

Let us now illustrate the concepts that we have learned up to now with a data set taken from the 1985 United States Statistical Abstracts. The data involve 1984 crime levels from all 50 states and the District of Columbia for 7 types of crimes. The 7 types of crime levels (the variables), were murder, forcible rape, robbery, aggravated assault, burglary, larceny-theft, and motor vehicle theft—measured for each state (the observations), in offenses per one hundred thousand population. Thus, we have a 51 × 7 data matrix, X. Although all variables are measured in the same metric, number of offenses per one hundred thousand, the variances of the variables ranged from 20.79 for murder, to 481,483 for larceny-theft. Therefore, the first principal component of the covariance matrix would be dominated by larceny-theft since this direction maximizes the variation. Consequently, it seems more reasonable, in this situation, to conduct a principal component analysis on the correlation matrix rather than the covariance matrix.

If the variables are all in the same metric and the variances do not differ widely from one another, then it might be reasonable to conduct a principal components analysis of the covariance matrix rather than the correlation matrix. In the present case, however, the ratio of the largest variance of 481,483 for theft to the smallest variance of 20.79 for murder is 23,159. Even though theft is much more prevalent than murder, its importance should not be such that its influence alone essentially determines the results of the principal components analysis. Two other alternatives come to mind. First, since the mean and variance are positively correlated, the variables could be subjected to a log transformation prior to the computation of the covariance matrix. Second, the crime variables could be weighted according to their relative importance on some key criterion (e.g., seriousness of crime) prior to computing the covariance matrix. The correlations among the seven variables are presented in Table 3.1.

The correlations among the variables are all high and we might suspect that a few principal components would explain most of the variation in the original seven crime variables. For example, if we were going to use this state-level crime data as part of a larger set of state-level social indicators, then tabular presentations would be greatly simplified by interpreting and reporting one or two principal

36

TABLE 3.1
Correlation Matrix for Seven Crime Indicators

	Murder	Rape	Robbery	Assault	Burglary	Larceny-Theft	MV Theft
Murder	1.000						
Rape	0.651	1.000					
Robbery	0.810	0.501	1.000				
Assault	0.821	0.707	0.722	1.000			
Burglary	0.593	0.740	0.552	0.686	1.000		
Larceny-Theft	0.434	0.641	0.480	0.557	0.751	1.000	
MV Theft	0.490	0.565	0.658	0.563	0.584	0.414	1.000

component scores rather than the seven variable scores. The latent roots and associated latent vectors are presented in Table 3.2.

The correlations of the variables with the principal components, sometimes referred to as component loadings, are obtained by multiplying the elements in a particular column in Table 3.2 by the square root of the corresponding latent root. The principal component loadings as well as the percent of variance explained by each principal component individually and cumulatively are presented in Table 3.3.

As we suspected, the first principal component had a large variance of 4.71 (Table 3.2) which accounted for $\left(\frac{4.71}{7}\times100\right)$ or 67.3% (Table 3.3) of the variance of the seven crime variables. The second and succeeding components accounted for considerably less variance ranging from 12% for the second principal component to 1.2% for the seventh (smallest) principal component. This pattern of latent roots is typical for highly correlated variables. The first principal component explains a substantial amount of variation in the variables and the remaining components considerably less. In addition, most or all of the variables have high correlations with the dominant principal component. The latent roots are ordered indicating that each succeeding principal component has less variance or, equivalently, explains less variation of the variables. The nature of principal components solutions for correlation matrices exhibiting various patterns of correlations will be discussed in a later section.

The problem now is to decide on how many principal components are needed to adequately represent the data. We previously discussed a number of criteria that are used to decide on how many principal components to retain. They are somewhat arbitrary and the use of different rules sometimes yields conflicting results.

TABLE 3.2

Latent Vectors and Corresponding Latent Roots from the
Correlation Matrix in Table 3.1

| | Principal Component | | | | | | |
	1	2	3	4	5	6	7
Murder	.389	.399	.414	.060	.039	.323	−.640
Rape	.387	−.272	.084	.644	.494	.162	.291
Robbery	.380	.462	−.060	−.489	.204	.218	.558
Assault	.410	.168	.288	.148	−.309	−.763	.151
Burglary	.394	−.385	−.054	−.013	−.708	.418	.130
Larceny-Theft	.341	−.590	.066	−.551	.339	−.218	−.257
MV Theft	.340	.169	−.853	.133	.021	−.144	−.298
Latent root (variance)	4.710	.837	.568	.397	.217	.186	.085

TABLE 3.3

Principal Component Loadings for Crime Variables and
Percent Variance Explained

| | Principal Component | | | | | | |
	1	2	3	4	5	6	7
Murder	0.845	0.365	0.312	0.038	0.018	0.139	−0.187
Rape	0.839	−0.249	0.063	0.406	0.230	0.070	0.085
Robbery	0.825	0.423	−0.045	−0.308	0.095	0.094	0.163
Assault	0.889	0.154	0.217	0.093	−0.144	−0.329	0.044
Burglary	0.855	−0.352	−0.041	−0.008	−0.330	0.180	0.038
Theft	0.739	−0.540	0.050	−0.347	0.158	−0.094	−0.075
MV Theft	0.738	0.155	−0.643	0.084	0.010	−0.062	−0.087
Percent variance explained individually	67.3%	12.0%	8.1%	5.7%	3.1%	2.7%	1.2%
Percent variance explained cumulatively	67.3%	79.2%	87.4%	93.0%	96.1%	98.8%	100%

The first component explains about two-thirds of the variance in
the seven crime variables. We can use either the latent vectors (Table
3.2) or the principal component loadings (Table 3.3) to interpret the
principal components since the two vectors are proportional to each

other. Relatively large elements in either vector indicate the variables that are important in defining a particular principal component. However, let us use the component loadings (correlations) to interpret the principal components.

The first principal component has large correlations with all seven crime variables. It is, therefore, interpreted as an overall crime dimension. If we were to create a principal component score using the elements of the first latent vector, it would be essentially an equally weighted average of the seven standardized crime scores. If the variables are all positively correlated, then the elements of the latent vector (or principal component loadings) are all positive. If the correlations are of about the same magnitude as they are in this example, then the elements of the first latent vector, or the loadings, are all positive and of about the same magnitude. The largest principal component in these circumstances is sometimes called a size factor. If we wanted only a single index that best summarized the data, then the first principal component is it. This is typically what we do when we construct an index such as a total test score. The test items are usually highly correlated and the correlations are of about the same magnitude. The information in the items is combined in an equally weighted composite of the items to yield a total test score. In situations where the correlations are homogeneous, an equally weighted composite of the variables would have an almost perfect correlation with the first principal component.

If we wanted to retain enough principal components to account for 80% of the variation, then two components would just about suffice since the first two components account for 79.2% of the total variation. The loadings of the second principal component have both positive (4) and negative signs (3). This is the expected pattern of the second and succeeding principal components if the first component has all positive correlations with the variables. The reason for this is that the first principal component must be orthogonal to all the remaining principal components. In order for this condition to be fulfilled, the sum of the cross products of the elements of the first latent vector with the elements of each of the remaining latent vectors must be equal to zero (i.e., $a_1'a_k = 0$ for $k = 1, 2, \ldots, p$). Since all of the elements of a_1 are positive, some of the elements in a_k must be negative for $a_1' a_k = 0$. Of course, the signs of any latent vector can be freely reversed since we can multiply both sides of $Ra = \lambda a$ by -1 and still maintain the equality.

When we have an overall size factor the succeeding principal components with alternating positive and negative signs are usually interpreted as contrasts. Our second principal component has high positive correlations (or large weights) with murder and robbery, both violent crimes, and high negative correlations (or large weights) with burglary and theft, both property crimes. Consequently we can interpret this principal component as a contrast between violent crimes and property crimes. That is, we add the violent crimes and subtract the property crimes to compute the second principal component score for a given state. The remaining three variables have smaller correlations or weights so they are given less weight in the interpretation. The negative loading of rape on the second principal component, although low, is somewhat puzzling since it has the same sign as the property crimes. It could be that some rapes are committed during a burglary or theft. The first few principal components are, in many instances, interpretable. They are the ones that explain most of the variation in the set of variables. Frequently, the smaller components are more difficult to interpret. Sometimes researchers prefer to rotate the retained components as in factor analysis. We will discuss this later on.

The sum of squares of all the loadings on a particular principal component is equal to the latent root (variance) associated with that component. This just indicates that the variance of a principal component is equal to the amount of variation that is explained across all of the variables. It is useful to examine the sum of squares of the loadings for each row of the principal component loading matrix as well because the row sum of squares indicates how much variance for that variable is accounted for by the retained principal components. For example, the proportion of variance in murder explained by the first two principal components is $(.845)^2 + (.365)^2$ or .847. Doing likewise for the remaining six rows, we have the proportion of variance that the first two principal components explain for each of the seven variables, as presented in Table 3.4.

Table 3.4 indicates that all the variables except motor vehicle theft have a substantial proportion of their variance explained by the largest two principal components. Motor vehicle theft had only 56.9% of it variance accounted for by the first two principal components whereas all but one of the remaining variables (e.g., rape) had over 80% of their variance explained by the first two principal components. If we wanted to explain at least 75% of the variation in each variable, then we would retain the third principal component as well since motor vehicle theft has a high correlation with the third component. In fact, squaring the motor vehicle loading of .643 on the third component and adding it to .569, the proportion of variance accounted for would increase from .569 to $.569 + (-.643)^2$ or .98. The

TABLE 3.4

Proportion of Variance Accounted for in Crime Variables
by First Two Principal Components

	Proportion of Variance Accounted for
1. murder	.847
2. rape	.766
3. robbery	.860
4. assault	.814
5. burglary	.855
6. theft	.838
7. motor vehicle theft	.569

variance accounted for in the remaining six variables would also increase by retaining the third component, but not to a large extent because their correlations with the third component are considerably
smaller. The number of components retained depends on the eventual
use of the principal components. If they were going to be used as independent variables in a regression analysis, then we might want to
retain three components so that all of the variables would be adequately represented by the principal components. We can always
eventually discard the components that do not significantly correlate
with the dependent variable.

Let us summarize the application of these criteria for deciding on
how many principal components to obtain. We begin by plotting the
latent roots in Figure 3.6. Kaiser's criterion calls for retaining only
the largest component. Jolliffe's criterion leads to the retention of two
components, but we may want to retain the third component because
motor vehicle theft is not adequately represented by the first two
components but is heavily represented by the third principal component. Using Cattell's scree criterion a steep slope is evident from the
first to the second latent roots and the second through the seventh
points can be fitted fairly well by a straight line of negligible slope.
Consequently, by this criterion, we would retain two components. The
various criteria and modifications thereof lead to the retention of one,
two, or three principal components. There are no hard and fast rules
and the various criteria can give conflicting results. However, three
components seem to be a reasonable choice. Three principal components account for 87% of the variation, represent all seven variables
well, and are readily interpretable.

We can compute the principal component scores for each of the 51
states by using the appropriate latent vectors. For example, the score

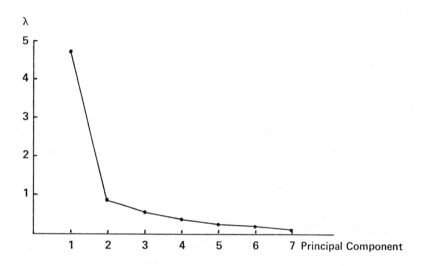

Figure 3.6: Plot of the Eigenvalues of the Crime Variable Correlation Matrix

on the first principal component for the state of Maine is .389(-1.080) + .387(-1.277) +. 380 (-.761) + .410(-1.030) + .394 (-.675) + .341(-.629) + .340(-.939) = -2.245, where the values in parentheses are standardized scores for the seven corresponding crime rates. Since the mean score for each principal component is zero, Maine has a low score on the first principal component.

The principal component scores for any pair of principal components can be plotted. The reasons for doing this include checking for outlying observations, searching for clusters and, in general, understanding the structure of the data. The principal component scores on the first two principal components are plotted in Figure 3.7 using SYSTAT® (Wilkinson, 1984). Before plotting, SYSTAT® standardizes the principal component scores so that each principal component has a standard deviation of 1. This means that the distance between points is no longer the Euclidian distance, but the Mahalanobis distance $(x_i - x_j)'R^{-1}(x_i - x_j)$, which takes into account the intercorrelations among the variables. Intuitively, it prevents double counting in that highly correlated variables which are, by definition, redundant are given less weight than lowly correlated variables in defining the distance between two points.

42

FACTOR (1)

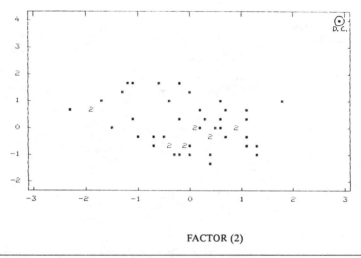

FACTOR (2)

Figure 3.7: Plot of the First Pair of Standardized Principal Components for

This plot will be discussed more fully when we discuss cluster analysis and outliers, but even a cursory examination of the plot indicates a clearly outlying observation, circled and identified as Washington, D.C., in the upper right hand corner of the plot.

4. DECOMPOSITION PROPERTIES OF THE PRINCIPAL COMPONENTS

This chapter describes two important decomposition properties. The principal components can be used both to decompose the variables into additive contributions from the components and to decompose the covariance (correlation) matrix into additive contributions from the components.

Decomposition of the Variables

We have seen that a vector of principal components scores can be expressed as $y = A'x$ where y is a $p \times 1$ vector of principal component scores, A' is the matrix of latent vectors arrayed in rows and x is the $p \times 1$ vector of variable scores. Since A' is an orthogonal matrix,

$AA' = I$ and we can premultiply the left and right side of $y = A'x$ by A to give $Ay = AA'x = x$. Thus, x, the vector of variables, can be expressed as a linear combination of the principal components, y, using A as the linear transformation matrix. Since $x = Ay$, it can also be expressed as $x = A_{(p \times k)}Y_{(k \times 1)} + A_{(p \times (p - k))}Y_{((p - k) \times 1)}$ where $A_{(p \times k)}$ is the matrix of latent vectors for the first k principal components that are retained, $y_{(k \times 1)}$ is the corresponding vector of principal component scores, $A_{(p \times (p - k))}$ is the matrix of latent vectors for the $p - k$ principal components that are discarded and $y_{((p - k) \times 1)}$ is the corresponding vector of principal component scores for the discarded components.

The above equation indicates that we can approximate x by using the first k principal components. The larger the k, the better the approximation of x. For our crime data, we retained the first three principal components so that $A_{(p \times k)}$ equals $A_{(7 \times 3)}$, the first three latent vectors, arrayed as columns. That is, we approximate the crime data by using the first three principal components. Thus, the variables x can be decomposed into additive contributions by the principal components. For example, in order to approximate x_1 (murder) for a particular state, we would multiply the score on principal component one by .389, multiply the score on principal component two by .399, multiply the score on principal component three by .414, and sum these products. We get these weights from Table 3.2.

Spectral Decomposition of the Correlation or Covariance Matrix

Another important decomposition is the decomposition of the covariance or correlation matrix with respect to the principal components. Since $x = Ay$, we have $xx'=Ayy'A'$. Taking the expectation of each side we have $E(xx') = R = AE(yy')A' = A \Lambda A'$ where Λ is a diagonal matrix of the latent roots of R or, equivalently, the variances of the principal components, y. In this derivation, we have assumed that x is a vector of standardized scores. The matrix expression $R = A \Lambda A'$ can be written as

$$R = \sum_{i=1}^{p} \lambda_i a_i a_i'.$$

This indicates that R can be decomposed into a sum of the contribution for each of the p principal components. From the form of the last equation, it can be seen that the large principal components (those with large λ's) make more of a contribution to R than the small principal components (those with small λ's).

For our crime data, the contribution of the first principal component to **R** is

$$\lambda_1 \, a_1 a_1' = 4.710 \begin{bmatrix} .389 \\ .387 \\ .380 \\ .410 \\ .394 \\ .341 \\ .340 \end{bmatrix} [.389, .387, .380, .410, .394, .341, .340]$$

$$= \begin{bmatrix} .713 & .709 & .696 & .751 & .722 & .625 & .623 \\ .709 & .705 & .693 & .747 & .718 & .622 & .620 \\ .696 & .693 & .680 & .734 & .705 & .610 & .609 \\ .751 & .747 & .734 & .792 & .761 & .659 & .657 \\ .722 & .718 & .705 & .761 & .731 & .633 & .631 \\ .625 & .622 & .610 & .659 & .633 & .548 & .546 \\ .623 & .620 & .609 & .657 & .631 & .546 & .544 \end{bmatrix}$$

while the contribution of the smallest principal component is

$$\lambda_7 \, a_7 a_7' = .085 \begin{bmatrix} -.640 \\ .291 \\ .558 \\ .151 \\ .130 \\ -.257 \\ -.248 \end{bmatrix} [-.640, .291, .558, .151, .130, -.257, -.248]$$

$$= \begin{bmatrix} .035 & -.016 & -.030 & -.008 & -.007 & .014 & .016 \\ -.016 & .007 & .014 & .004 & -.003 & -.006 & -.007 \\ -.030 & .014 & .026 & .007 & .006 & -.012 & -.014 \\ -.008 & .004 & .007 & .002 & .002 & -.003 & -.004 \\ -.007 & .003 & .006 & .002 & .001 & -.003 & -.003 \\ .014 & -.006 & -.012 & -.003 & -.003 & .006 & .007 \\ .016 & -.007 & -.014 & -.004 & -.003 & .007 & .008 \end{bmatrix}$$

It can be seen that the elements $\lambda_1 a_1 a_1'$ associated with the first principal component are very large compared to the elements associated with the smallest principal component $\lambda_7 a_7 a_7'$. In fact, $\lambda_1 a_1 a_1'$ is a rough approximation to R. We have already defined the loading (correlations) of the variables on the ith principal component 1_i, as $\sqrt{\lambda_i}\, a_i$.

Consequently, R can also be decomposed as $R = \sum_{i=1}^{p} l_i l_i'$.

5. PRINCIPAL COMPONENTS OF PATTERNED CORRELATION MATRICES

The pattern of latent roots and their associated latent vectors depends on the pattern of correlations. For well-defined correlational structures (e.g., variables falling into clearly defined clusters with high correlations within clusters and low correlations between clusters), the pattern of latent roots readily indicates the number of principal components to retain, and those that are retained are easily interpreted from the latent vectors or, equivalently, the loadings. If the pattern of correlations has no well defined structure, then this lack of structure will be reflected in the principal components. They will be difficult to interpret.

In the hypothetical case in which the correlations within a cluster are exactly equal and the correlations between clusters are exactly zero, there is a principal component associated with each cluster whose latent root is $1 + (p_i - 1)\rho_i$ where p_i is the number of variables in the ith cluster of variables and ρ_i is the common correlation among the variables in the ith cluster. There are $p_i - 1$ remaining latent roots associated with the ith cluster, each one equal to $1 - \rho_i$.

The latent vector associated with the ith cluster of variables has an equal element (or loading) for each of the variables comprising the cluster; the remaining elements are zero. Such correlation matrices have a block diagonal form such as the matrix in Table 5.1.

Variables 1 through 3 in Table 5.1 form one cluster, and variables 4 through 7 form another. The latent root associated with the first cluster (variables 1 – 3) is $1 + (3 - 1).80$ or 2.60 and its associated normed latent vector is [$1/\sqrt{3}$, $1/\sqrt{3}$, $1/\sqrt{3}$,0,0,0,0]. The latent root associated with the second cluster (variables 4–7) is $1 + (4 - 1).70$ or 3.1 and its associated latent vector is [0, 0, 0, 1/2, 1/2, 1/2, 1/2]. The proportion of total variance accounted for by the first two principal components is $(2.6 + 3.1)/7$ or .81. There are five remaining latent roots, two associated with the first cluster and three associated with the second cluster. The two remaining latent roots associated with the first cluster are both equal to $1 - .80$ or .20. The three remaining latent roots associated with the second cluster are equal to $1 - .70$ or .30.

TABLE 5.1
Block Diagonal Correlation Matrix

	Variables						
	1	2	3	4	5	6	7
1	1.00	.80	.80	0	0	0	0
2	.80	1.00	.80	0	0	0	0
3	.80	.80	1.00	0	0	0	0
4	0	0	0	1.00	.70	.70	.70
5	0	0	0	.70	1.00	.70	.70
6	0	0	0	.70	.70	1.00	.70
7	0	0	0	.70	.70	.70	1.00

All of the principal components associated with these five roots would be discarded by any of the criteria discussed above. The elements of the latent vectors of these roots involve contrasts (i.e., a mixture of positive and negative signs) among the variables comprising the cluster. However, because of sphericity, the latent vectors are not unique and, hence, we would not want to interpret them anyway.

In practice, this ideal situation never occurs, but if the correlations within a cluster of variables are fairly homogeneous, and the correlations among variables across clusters are relatively low, then we can use the above principles to approximate a principal components solution. We just replace ρ_i in the above formula with $\overline{\rho}_i$, the average of the correlations within the ith variable cluster.

If all of the variables are equally correlated, then we have one large principal component with latent root equal to $1 + (p - 1)\rho$ where p is the total number of variables and ρ is the common correlation among the variables. The associated latent vector has p elements each equal to $1/\sqrt{p}$. The remaining $p - 1$ latent roots are all equal to $1 - \rho$. For example, the largest latent root of a 10×10 correlation matrix with a common correlation of .50 is $1 + (10 - 1).50$ or 5.5. The remaining nine latent roots are each equal to $1 - .50$ or .50. The nine latent vectors associated with them are arbitrary and would be discarded by any criterion.

Example

Let us take another example. Woodward, Retka, and Ng (1984) present the intercorrelations of seven heroin abuse indicators measured for 24 major metropolitan areas across the nation. The heroin abuse indicators were the number of emergency room episodes due to heroin overdoses (ER); the number of medical examiner episodes indicating death due to heroin overdose (D); the number of heroin users admitted to treatment (T); the number of arrests where opioid was involved (Arr); the number of pharmacy thefts where opioid was stolen (Ph.T); the retail price of heroin (Pr); and the retail purity of heroin (Pur). The correlations among these seven indicators are presented in Table 5.2.

A cursory examination of the correlation matrix in Table 5.2 indicates that the first five variables are all highly intercorrelated, but have relatively low correlations with the last two variables (price and purity of heroin). The latter two variables have a moderate negative correlation of −.382. This pattern of correlations indicates two clusters of variables and suggests that two principal components might be adequate for accounting for variation in the seven heroin abuse indicators.

The principal component loadings, latent roots, and percentage of variance accounted for are shown in Table 5.3. Using both Kaiser's and Jolliffe's criteria, two principal components would be retained. If we plotted the eigenvalues, then Cattell's criterion would suggest retaining three principal components since the points for components 3 through 7 fall approximately on a straight line with slope considerably less than the slope of the line joining the second and third components.

Two components account for 77% of the variation. In addition, each indicator has a high loading on at least one component so that each indicator is adequately represented by the first two principal components although some indicators are better represented than others. For example, the first two principal components explain $(.924)^2 + (.253)^2$ or 92.7% of the variation in treatment admissions (Tr), but only $(-.694)^2 + (.448)^2$ or 68.2% of the variation in heroin purity (Pur). In selecting two components we have used Jolliffe's criterion augmented by a check to make sure that each variable is adequately represented. For many cases, all variables are adequately represented using Jolliffe's criterion, but it needs checking.

The first principal component has high loadings on the five indicators which reflect prevalence. Since the loadings are proportional to the elements in the latent vector, this component is essentially an average of the five prevalence indicators. The second principal component has a high positive loading for price and a high negative loading for purity. It is a contrast between price and purity. Those SMSAs which have high scores on the second component are characterized by high heroin prices and low purity. Those with low scores are charac-

TABLE 5.2
Intercorrelations of Seven Heroin Abuse Indicators

	Er	D	T	Ph.T	Arr	Pr	Pur
Er	1.000						
D	0.690	1.000					
T	0.861	0.822	1.000				
Ph.T	0.724	0.671	0.810	1.000			
Arr	0.738	0.543	0.648	0.604	1.000		
Pr	−0.148	0.032	0.032	0.019	−0.190	1.000	
Pur	0.253	0.250	0.205	0.307	0.496	−0.382	1.000

TABLE 5.3
Principal Components Loading Matrix for Heroin Indicator
Correlation Matrix

	Principal Component						
	1	2	3	4	5	6	7
Er	0.907	0.054	−0.233	−0.180	0.017	0.259	0.140
D	0.835	0.221	−0.014	0.373	0.305	−0.124	0.077
Tr	0.924	0.253	−0.110	0.067	−0.005	0.107	−0.231
Ph.T	0.862	0.159	0.068	0.085	−0.446	−0.137	0.054
Arr	0.825	−0.224	0.115	−0.440	0.152	−0.196	−0.024
Pr	−0.129	0.840	0.506	−0.121	0.043	0.065	0.020
Pur	0.448	−0.694	0.529	0.144	−0.002	0.130	−0.005
Latent root	4.017	1.378	.621	.412	.317	0.172	.083
Percent variance	57.38	19.69	8.87	5.89	4.53	2.46	1.19
Cumulative percent	57.38	77.07	85.94	91.83	96.36	98.82	100.00

terized by low prices and high purity. The second principal component can be interpreted as a heroin availability index reflecting illicit drug market forces.

6. ROTATION OF PRINCIPAL COMPONENTS

Even though the retained principal components may be interpretable, some researchers prefer to rotate the principal components as is typically done in factor analysis. An orthogonal rotation is just a shift (rotation) to a new set of coordinate axes in the same subspace spanned by the principal components.

If most of the observations lie near a plane in the variable space, then principal components analysis will find the two coordinate axes, the principal components, that define the plane of closest fit to the essentially two dimensional swarm of points. However, any two other perpendicular coordinate axes lying in the same plane can also be used to describe the observations without any loss of information. Like the principal components, the new coordinate axes are also defined by their correlations (loadings) with the original variables, but hopefully the pattern of loadings on the rotated coordinated axes will be more conceptually appealing, thus allowing for a simpler interpretation of the rotated components.

Varimax rotation (Kaiser, 1958) is probably the most popular orthogonal rotation procedure. By orthogonal rotation we mean that the new coordinate axes, like the principal component axes, are perpendicular to one another. In varimax, the coordinate axes are rotated so as to maximize what is called the varimax criterion. Thus, like the principal components solution, the varimax solution is unique. The varimax criteria maximizes the sum of the variances of the squared loadings within each column of the loading matrix. That is, the varimax criteria results in a new set of orthogonal coordinate axes where each new coordinate axis has either large or small loadings of the variables on it. Since the rotated loading matrix is an orthogonal transformation of the original principal components loading matrix, it can be expressed as $L_r = LT$ where L_r is the $p \times k$ rotated loading matrix, L is the original $p \times k$ principal component loading matrix, and T is the $k \times k$ orthogonal transformation matrix that maximizes the varimax criterion. Kaiser proposed an iterative algorithm to find T. Rotation will be further discussed in a subsequent section comparing principal components and factor analysis.

Example

We will illustrate rotation by taking the loadings on the two principal components of the satisfaction variables from Table 3.1 and subjecting them to a varimax rotation. The result is the rotated loading matrix presented in Table 6.1. Note that each rotated component has either very high or very low loadings by the variables. The first rotated component has very high loadings by the three job-related satisfaction measures and very low loadings by the two health-care satisfaction measures. We would interpret this rotated component as job satisfaction. The second rotated component has very high loadings by the two health care satisfaction measures and very low load-

TABLE 6.1
Rotated Components for Military Satisfaction Variables

Variables	Rotated Components 1	2
Satisfaction with Job (SJ)	.835	.034
Satisfaction with Job Training (SJT)	.751	.180
Satisfaction with Working Conditions (SWC)	.790	.185
Satisfaction with Medical Care (SMC)	.182	.878
Satisfaction with Dental Care (SDC)	.107	.896
Variance Explained $(\sum_{j=1}^{5} r_{ij}^2, i = 1, 2)$	1.931	1.641

ings by the three job-related satisfaction measures. This rotated component would be interpreted as health care satisfaction. The amount of variance explained by each rotated component is the sum of the squared loadings shown as the last row in Table 6.1. The total amount of variation explained by the two rotated components is 1.931 + 1.641 = 3.52—the same amount of variation explained by the original principal components. This makes sense logically since the rotated coordinate axes lie in the same plane defined by the original principal component axes.

Since both the unrotated and rotated solutions explain exactly the same amount of variation in the variables, the choice between the two hinges upon their interpretability from the researcher's perspective. Each solution is unique with respect to maximizing their respective mathematical criteria. The original principal components solution maximizes the sum of the squared loadings while the varimax rotated solution maximizes, as its name implies, a variance like function of the loading with the components.

7. USING PRINCIPAL COMPONENTS TO SELECT A SUBSET OF VARIABLES

Principal components analysis can be useful in selecting a subset of variables to represent the total set of variables. This discussion does not take into account the use of outside criteria, such as their effectiveness in predicting a particular dependent variable, to select the subset of variables; only the internal structure of the data is considered. Subsequently, we will consider the joint use of outside criteria as well as the principal components in the selection of variables as independent variables in regression analyses.

The rationale for selecting a subset of variables to represent the variation in a set of variables rather than the principal components themselves is based on two considerations. First, in order to compute the principal component scores, we need measures of all variables in the variable set since each principal component is a linear combination of all of the variables. Some variables may be too difficult or too expensive to measure, and, therefore, collecting data on them in future studies may be impractical. Second, while the variables themselves are usually readily interpretable, the principal components are sometimes uninterpretable. This is not a serious drawback, however, since, as we have seen, the principal components can be rotated to a more interpretable structure by varimax or other rotation algorithms.

If the correlations among the variables are high, or if there are clusters of variables with high intercorrelations, then, in many instances, we can represent the variation in the total set of variables by a much smaller subset of variables. McCabe (1984) calls these principal variables. There are a number of strategies for selecting a subset of variables using principal components analyses. They are summarized in more detail by Jolliffe (1986).

The first step is to decide how many variables to select. One approach is to use Jolliffe's criteria of $\lambda = .70$ to determine which principal components to retain. Then one variable can be selected to represent each of the retained principal components. The variable that has the highest loading or weight on a principal component would be selected to represent that component, provided it has not been chosen to represent a larger variance principal component. In that case, the variable with the next largest loading would be chosen. The procedure would start with the largest principal component and proceed to the smallest retained component.

Another approach is to use the discarded principal components to discard variables. We would start with the smallest discarded component and delete the variable with the largest weight or loading on that component. Then the variable with the largest loading on the second smallest component would be discarded. If the variable had been previously discarded, then the variable with the next highest loading would be discarded. This procedure continues up through the largest discarded component. The rationale for deleting variables with high weights on small components is that small components reflect redundancies among the variables with high weights. Another way to look at it is that components with small variances are unimportant and therefore variables that load highly on them are likewise unimportant.

Example

Let us apply both of these approaches to the crime data example whose principal components are presented in Table 3.3. If we retain two components, then assault would be selected to represent the first component (overall crime level) and theft would be selected to represent the second component (property crimes versus violent crimes). If we use the five discarded principal components to discard five variables, then working from the smallest to the largest principal component we would discard in order murder, assault, burglary, rape, and motor vehicle theft. We are left with robbery and theft as the selected variables. Both of these two variable sets had theft, a property crime, in common. Even though the second variable differed, they both represented violent crimes, robbery and assault. Jolliffe (1986) discusses a number of criteria that can be used to evaluate the efficiency of particular subsets of variables in representing the total set of variables. One criterion that can be used is the total amount of variation the selected variables explain. The total amount of variation that a subset of variables explains is the sum of the variation they explain in each of the discarded variables in addition to the sum of the variances for the variables comprising the subset.

Each discarded variable is regressed on the retained variables and the corresponding squared multiple correlations are summed. If we add to that the variances of the retained variables, which, in this case, are each 1, then we have a measure of the total variation that is accounted for by the variable subset. This formula can be expressed as

$$n_r + \sum_{i=1}^{d} R_{i,r}^2$$

where n_r is the number of retained variables and $R_{i,r}^2$ is the squared multiple correlation of the ith discarded variable with the r retained variables. Assault and theft were selected as a two variable subset from our first approach. The total variance accounted for by these two variables is $2 + .675 + .588 + .530 + .668 + .332$ or 4.793, where .675, .588, .530, .668, and .332 are the squared multiple correlations of murder, rape, robbery, burglary, and motor vehicle theft, respectively, with assault and theft.

The total amount of variation explained by the two largest principal components is 5.54 or 79.2% of the variation in the seven crime variables. The total amount of variation explained by our two variable subset (assault and theft) is 4.793 or 68.5% (100 × 4.793/7). The largest two principal components explain more of the total variation than any subset of two variables because the directions of the principal component coordinate axes are defined as those directions which maximize the total variation accounted for in the set of variables. No other set of coordinate axes accounts for as much variability. The coordinate axis of the two variables approximate the direction of the principal component axes but do not define exactly the same two-dimensional subspace. Nevertheless, the two variable subset compares favorably with the first two principal components with respect to the percent of variance accounted for, 68.5% for the variables versus 79.2% for the components.

If we want a subset of variables that will explain at least as much variation as the first two principal components, then we need a subset of variables larger than two. Since the correlations among the variables are high, increasing the subset from two to three should satisfy this requirement. A logical selection for the third variable of the subset is motor vehicle theft which has the highest loading on the third principal component. Regressing murder, rape, robbery, and burglary on assault, theft, and motor vehicle theft we find R^2s of .677, .613, .616, and .699, respectively. Thus, the total amount of variance explained by our three variable subset of assault, theft, and motor vehicle theft is $3 + .677 + .613 + .616 + .699$ or 5.605. This is a little larger than the total variance of 5.54 accounted for by the first two components. So three variables explain a little more variation than the two largest principal components (80.1% versus 79.2%). The three variable subset, however, does not explain as much variation as the first three largest principal components. The first three components account for 87.4% of the variation as contrasted to 80.1% for our three variable subset.

Let us now examine the total variability accounted for by our two variable subset (robbery and theft) selected by our second approach, discarding variables associated with small principal components. The squared multiple correlations of murder, rape, assault, burglary, and motor vehicle theft with robbery and theft were .659, .459, .580, .612, and .445, respectively. The total variability explained by robbery and theft is, therefore, $2 + .659 + .459 + .580 + .612 + .445 = 4.755$. In this case the second approach performed almost as well as the first approach (67.9% versus 68.5% of the variation explained). The sec-

54

ond approach yields robbery, theft, and motor vehicle theft as a three variable subset. Two of these variables (theft and motor vehicle theft) are in common with the three variable subset selected by the first approach. The total variation in the seven variables explained by this three variable subset is 5.426 or 77.5% of the variation. This is a little less than the 80.1% explained by the three variable subset selected by the first approach.

The specific finding here that the first approach is preferable to the second does not mean that this holds in general. In addition, there could be other variable subsets of the same size that account for a larger percentage of the total variability. There are more complex approaches (see Jolliffe, 1986) based on these fundamental principles. The simple approaches discussed here (selected subsets of variables that had conceptual appeal in that they were highly correlated with the principal components), did a good job in representing the total variation in the variable set. Another possibility is to rotate the retained components before using the first approach to select the variable subset. Rotating the first two principal components, we find that robbery and theft had the highest loadings on rotated components one and two, respectively; the same two variable subset that was selected by the second approach of discarding variables.

We may also want to consider a compromise approach lying between selecting a single variable to represent each important principal component and computing the principal component scores which involves using information in all of the variables. The compromise is to represent each important principal component as an equally weighted composite of, say, two, three, or four variables whose loadings exceed some cutoff value such as .40 or .50. This is equivalent to giving a weight of 1 to variables important in defining the principal component and a weight of zero to the less important variables. Simple weighting schemes like this often produce approximate component scores that hold up better under cross-validation than the exact component scores. In addition, we just need a subset of the variables to calculate the "component" scores. This approach is particularly advantageous if the variables in the set are based upon unreliable measures since a composite of unreliable variables can be considerably more reliable than any single variable making up the composite.

8. PRINCIPAL COMPONENTS VERSUS FACTOR ANALYSIS

While both principal components and factor analysis have the common aim of reducing the dimensionality of a variable set, there are some important differences between the two techniques. The most important difference is that principal components analysis decomposes the total variance as we have repeatedly emphasized. In the case of standardized variables, it produces a decomposition of R. We saw earlier that R can be decomposed into the product of three matrices $A \Lambda A'$ where A is the matrix of the latent vectors R arrayed as columns, A' is its transpose (latent vectors arrayed as rows) and Λ is a diagonal matrix of the associated latent roots of R. Because Λ is a diagonal matrix, we saw that this could also be written as

$$\sum_{i=1}^{p} \lambda_i a_i a_i'.$$

We defined the principal component loadings, the correlations of the variables with the components, as $\lambda_i^{1/2} a_i = l_i$ so that in terms of l_i, R can be decomposed as

$$\sum_{i=1}^{p} l_i l_i'$$

or LL' where L is the principal component loading matrix with principal components as columns and L' is its transpose. We can approximate R to any degree desired by retaining k principal components and discarding the remaining $p-k$. In this way R can be approximated as

$$\begin{array}{cc} L & L' \\ (p \times k) & (k \times p) \end{array}$$

Factor analysis, on the other hand, finds a decomposition of the reduced correlation matrix $R-U$ where U is a diagonal matrix of the unique variances associated with the variables. Unique variances are that part of each variable's variance that has nothing in common with the remaining $p-1$ variables. If we subtract the unique variances from 1, the elements in the principal diagonal of R, we have what are referred to as communalities in the principal diagonal of the reduced correlation matrix. The communality for each variable is the portion of the total variance that is shared with the remaining $p-1$ variables, or stated another way, the variance that a particular variable has in common with the remaining $p-1$ variables. The reduced correlation matrix with communalities in the principal diagonal instead of ones will be referred to as R_c. Factor analysis seeks a decomposition of R_c in terms of a $p \times k$ factor loading matrix L_f with the smallest k such that $R_c = L_f L_f'$. Usually k is much smaller than p. This contrasts with principal components analysis where L must be a $p \times p$ matrix in order for the principal components to fit R perfectly (i.e., for $R = LL'$). In factor analysis it is theoretically possible to find a $p \times k$ factor loading matrix L_f where k is much smaller than p that fits R_c perfectly. Communalities have to be estimated just like the factor loading matrix, L_f. An initial estimate, as we shall see, is the squared multiple correlation of each variable with the $p - 1$ remaining variables.

Since the principal components, y, equal $A'x$ and A' is a nonsingular matrix whose inverse is A, $x = Ay$. Thus, the principal components can be expressed as linear functions of the variables or the variables can be expressed as linear functions of the principal components. This is not the case in factor analysis since factor analysis, as we shall see, concentrates on defining the variables as a linear combination of common factors and unique factors. Contrary to principal components analysis, the factor analysis model does not provide a unique transformation from variables to factors.

Principal components analysis is a procedure to decompose the correlation matrix without regard to an underlying model. Most importantly, it does not distinguish between common variance and unique variance as factor analysis does. Factor analysis, on the other hand, has an underlying model that rests on a number of assumptions. The key assumption is that the ith variable in the variable set, x_i, can be expressed as a linear combination of hypothetical unobservable common factors plus a factor unique to that variable. Note that the emphasis here is on explaining x_i as a linear function of unobservable common factors while the emphasis in principal component analysis is expressing the principal component as a linear function of the x_i. The model assumes that the standardized variable x_i can be expressed as

$$\sum_{j=1}^{k} l_{ij} f_j + u_i$$

where l_{ij} is the loading of the ith variable on the jth factor, f_j is the factor score for the jth factor, and u_i is the unique factor score for the ith variable.

The object of factor analysis is to estimate the loadings l_{ij} which together form the factor loading matrix L_f which has p rows corresponding to variables and k columns corresponding to factors where k is considerably smaller than p. In order to estimate L_f, a number of assumptions have to be made. These assumptions are as follows: the mean and variance of f_j equal zero and one, respectively for all j; the correlations among the common factors are zero; the correlations between the common factors and the unique factors are zero, and the correlations between the p unique factors are all zero.

The model and its assumptions can be expressed in matrix algebra as $x = Lf + u$ where x is a vector of p standardized variables, L is the $p \times k$ factor loading matrix, f is a vector of k factor scores, and u is a vector of the p unique factor scores. This equation has the form of a regression equation. If we knew f for each individual then we could estimate L by least squares. However, f is hypothetical so we must use our other assumptions previously discussed to estimate L. Expressed in matrix algebra, they are $E(f) = E(u) = O$; $E(ff') = I$; $E(uu')$ is a diagonal matrix U; and $E(uf') = O$, where E is the expectation operator which is analogous to the operation of computing averages and the averages of cross products for sample data. We can then use these assumptions to show that $R = LL' + U$.

The assumption that $E(ff') = I$, i.e., the factors are uncorrelated, can be relaxed to allow the factors to be correlated. In our subsequent discussion of rotation we will see that L, the factor loading matrix, is not unique. It can be linearly transformed, by a transformation matrix, to another matrix L_r of the same dimensions. Geometrically, this is a rotation of the factor coordinate axes in the same common factor space. We can keep the axes perpendicular to one another using a rigid rotation which will result in uncorrelated factors or we can use a nonrigid rotation where the factor axes are allowed to form oblique angles to one another resulting in correlated factors. Factor analysis with correlated factors is sometimes called oblique factor analysis. In oblique factor analysis we also have to estimate Θ, the matrix of factor intercorrelations, as well as L. For oblique factor analysis, it can be shown that R can be decomposed as $L\Theta L' + U$.

There are a number of ways to estimate U and hence the reduced correlation matrix R_c. Once we have an estimate of R_c, then we can use the principal components algorithm to find L. Principal components analysis is usually used in two ways to estimate the factor loading matrix for the factor analysis model. One method is called iterative principal components analysis. It begins with a principal component analysis of the standard correlation matrix. The eigenvalues are examined and used, along with other considerations, to determine the number of factors accounting for the correlations among the variables. Kaiser's criteria of retaining components with eigenvalues equal or greater than one is often used, but other considerations, as we discussed earlier, can also be used. There are also statistical goodness of fit tests that can be used to determine how well a given number of factors fits the correlation matrix. For more details on determining the number of factors the reader is referred to Kim and Mueller (1978a, 1978b) and Harman (1976).

The number of common factors is determined and an initial communality estimate for each variable is obtained by summing the square of the loadings for the retained components. That is, we compute the sum of squares of the principal component loadings on the retained components for each row (variable) of the loading matrix. Then, these initial communality estimates are substituted for the ones in the principal diagonal of the correlation matrix for an initial estimate of the reduced correlation matrix, R_c. Then a second principal components analysis is done on R_c. Revised communality estimates for each variable are generated from this second component analysis by summing the squared loading on the k largest components where k is the number of common factors determined from the first principal component analysis. These revised communality estimates are now placed in the principal diagonal and a second principal component analysis is conducted on our revised reduced correlation matrix. New communality estimates are generated, and the new reduced correlation matrix is subjected to a third principal component analysis. The procedure continues until the factor loading matrices converge. That is, it continues until all of the corresponding elements of the factor loading matrices for the nth and the $(n + 1)$th principal component analysis are sufficiently close to one another (e.g., a difference of less than .001). Most standard statistical packages have an option for estimating the common factor analysis model by iterated principal components analysis.

Another option available in most standard packages is to replace the 1's in the principal diagonal of the correlation matrix with squared multiple correlations. Each variable is regressed upon the remaining p – 1 variables, and the corresponding squared multiple correlation replaces the 1 in the appropriate position on the principal diagonal. Since the communality is defined as the amount of variance shared with the remaining variables, this seems like a reasonable procedure (Guttman, 1956). A principal component analysis is then conducted on the reduced correlation matrix for estimating the factor loading matrix. The analysis needs only to be done once, an advantage over the iterated principal components analysis procedure. Both procedures give similar results.

There are other factor analysis procedures besides principal components factor analysis. A commonly used alternative approach is maximum likelihood factor analysis (Lawley and Maxwell, 1971). Maximum likelihood factor analysis assumes that the p variables have a multivariate normal distribution whereas principal components factor analysis requires no distributional assumptions. The estimated matrices L, U, and possibly Θ contain the respective estimated parameters which are most likely to have generated the sample data. In maximum likelihood factor analysis we have to specify the number of factors to be extracted. We might also provide certain information about L or the other parameter matrices as discussed below. The initial maximum likelihood estimates can also be rotated. The initial maximum likelihood and principal factor analysis solution tend to be similar. For a brief discussion of maximum likelihood factor analysis as well as other factoring techniques see Kim and Mueller (1978a and 1978b).

If we do not have a particular underlying model of the data in mind, then principal components can be useful in exploring the structure of a data set (e.g., searching for multivariate outliers, and visually clustering observations). It can also be used as an adjunct to other multivariate analysis procedures (e.g., addressing the problem of multicollinearity in regression analysis). Of course, it can be used directly to construct linear composites in order to both simplify the description of a data set and to be used as independent and dependent variables in further analyses.

On the other hand, if the variables contain a substantial amount of measurement error, which is often the case in the behavioral and social sciences, and we can postulate an underlying factor model for the data, then factor analysis has a decided advantage over principal components analysis. The common factors are uncontaminated by measurement error because measurement error is part of the unique variance which is uncorrelated with the common variance. Since, in this case, the principal components will be linear composites of unreliable variables, the principal components will contain measurement error.

While factor analysis can also be exploratory in the sense that nothing need be postulated with respect to either the number of factors or the pattern of variable loadings on these factors, there has been a recent move toward confirmatory factor analysis. Confirmatory factor analysis involves testing specific hypotheses about the underlying factor analysis model with respect to both the number of factors and the pattern of loadings (but not the actual numerical estimates) on each factor. With these constraints, the factor analysis model can be estimated by maximum likelihood and its fit to the observed covariance or correlation matrix can be evaluated in terms of a Chi-square goodness of fit statistic (Long, 1983). Both principal components and factor analysis give similar results if the communalities of the variables are high and/or there are a large number of variables.

Example

Let us illustrate the principal components factor analysis procedure on the crime data using the correlation matrix from Table 3.1. The two largest eigenvalues are 4.710 and .837. This suggests, according to Kaiser, that one common factor would adequately account for the intercorrelations among the crime variables. However, other researchers, using other criteria besides the size of the latent root, might prefer a two factor solution. We will accept two factors, in part, so that we can compare the principal factor analysis solution to the principal components analysis solution previously obtained.

We will estimate communalities by squared multiple correlations. The squared multiple correlations for murder, rape, robbery, assault, burglary, theft, and motor vehicle theft were .831, .710, .800, .756, .727, .640, and .606, respectively. For example, the R^2 of .831 for murder was obtained from regressing murder on the remaining six variables and so on for the remaining six R^2's. These R^2's are fairly high indicating that all seven variables share a high proportion of common variance. Murder has the highest communality, .831, and motor vehicle theft the lowest, .606. Using the R^2's as communality estimates to replace the ones on the principal diagonal of the correlation matrix from Table 3.1, we obtain the reduced correlation matrix presented in Table 8.1.

The principal components analysis of the reduced correlation matrix resulted in the factor loading matrix shown in Table 8.2. The latent roots or, equivalently, the amount of variance explained is also shown. Comparing Tables 3.3 and 8.2, there are a number of differences to be noted between the principal components analysis (Table 3.3) and the factor analysis (Table 8.2) results. First of all, the factors, individually and jointly, explain less of the total variance in the seven crime variables than the principal components.

TABLE 8.1
Reduced Correlation Matrix for Crime Variables

		1	2	3	4	5	6	7
1	MURDER	0.831						
2	RAPE	0.651	0.710					
3	ROBBERY	0.810	0.501	0.800				
4	ASSAULT	0.821	0.707	0.722	0.756			
5	BURGLARY	0.593	0.740	0.552	0.686	0.727		
6	THEFT	0.434	0.641	0.480	0.557	0.751	0.640	
7	MV THEFT	0.490	0.565	0.658	0.563	0.584	0.414	0.606

TABLE 8.2
Factor Loading Matrix for Crime Variables

Variable	Factor	
	1	2
MURDER	0.841	0.340
RAPE	0.810	−0.228
ROBBERY	0.814	0.368
ASSAULT	0.868	0.113
BURGLARY	0.828	−0.313
THEFT	0.702	−0.392
MV THEFT	0.696	0.051
latent root	4.443	.571
percent total variance explained	63.5%	8.2%
percent cumulative variance	63.5%	71.7%

The first principal component (Table 3.3) accounts for 67.3% of the total variance, whereas the first common factor (Table 8.2) accounts for 63.5% of the total variance. Similarly, the second principal component (Table 3.3) accounts for 12% of the total variance while the second common factor (Table 8.2) only accounts for 8.2% of the total variance. Together the first two principal components account for 79.2% of the total variance while the two common factors account for 71.7%.

It should be remembered that factor analysis is concerned with explaining common variance and not total variance. Thus, although the two common factors only account for 72% of the total variance, they, by definition, account for almost all of the common variance. They will not, in general, account for 100% of the common variance in an empirical data set because of sampling fluctuations. If a factor analysis model accounts for 100% of the common variance, then the off diagonal elements in the correlation matrix (i.e., the correlations) can be exactly reconstructed from the factor loading matrix (i.e., $R-U=LL'$). This will rarely be the case. However, the deviations of the correlations from the correlations predicted by the factor model (i.e., residuals) should be small enough to be explained as sampling fluctuations if we are to conclude that the factor analysis model fits the data. As mentioned previously, maximum likelihood factor analysis allows us to statistically test the goodness of fit of a particular factor analysis model to a sample correlation or covariance matrix.

Since the total variance explained by a component or factor is equal to the sum of squares of the loadings for the corresponding column, the principal component loadings will be higher, in general, than the factor loadings. While the principal component loadings are not much larger, in general, there are some noticeable differences. For example, theft has a loading of −.540 on the second principal component but only has a loading of −.392 on the second common factor. While there are differences in the two solutions, overall the differences are not great. This is because the communalities were large, in general, and did not differ substantially from one another. In cases where the communalities approach 1, then principal components analysis can be used as an approximation to factor analysis. However, when the communalities are small or vary considerably, then the two solutions will be quite different. In the case of generally small and varying communalities, the principal component loadings will be considerably larger than the factor loading and, in addition, the ranking of the size of principal component loadings for a particular component may be quite different from the rankings of the factor loadings on the corresponding factor (i.e., the principal component loadings will not be proportional to the corresponding factor loadings).

As the number of variables increases, the ratio of off-diagonal to diagonal elements becomes large and, consequently the size of the communalities, the diagonal elements, will have little effect on the solution. Factor analysis and principal components analysis will yield similar results. That is, the pattern of the two loading matrices will be the same. Each column of one loading matrix will be proportional to the corresponding column of the other. However, the principal component loadings will be larger than the factor loadings because the former is attempting to account for the total variation and the latter for the smaller amount of common variation.

Factor Rotation

We previously discussed the fact that the investigator can rotate the retained principal components if he prefers. This is sometimes done if the unrotated components are difficult to interpret. It also illustrates the fact that there is not a unique orthogonal decomposition of the correlation or covariance matrix. However, the principal components analysis decomposition is unique in that each succeeding component has maximal variance. Equivalently, the sum of the squared loading for each component is maximized. This desirable mathematical property, especially if the components are readily interpretable, precludes the need for rotation.

In factor analysis, the initial factor solution, which also has optimal properties with respect to successive maximization of explained common variance, is considered arbitrary and there is the need to transform the original solution to a rotated solution that has desirable properties with respect to the simplicity and interpretability of the rotated factor loading matrix. Rotations, like principal components analysis, optimize a particular mathematical criterion that results in a rotated factor loading matrix with certain desirable properties sometimes called simple structure (Thurstone, 1947).

Rotation brings about simple structure by either simplifying the rows (variables) or columns (factors) of the rotated factor loading matrix. Varimax rotation, as discussed earlier, simplifies the columns of the factor loading matrix by maximizing the variance of the squared loadings. It results in a unique rotated factor loading matrix. That is, there is only a single unique factor loading matrix that maximizes the varimax criterion. Other definitions of simple structure have been defined analytically for computer implementation (Harman, 1976). Each definition leads to a different unique factor loading matrix, although there may be similarities among them. Varimax, by far, is the most commonly used rotation algorithm. The point is that while L is not unique, it is unique with respect to a particular analytical criterion. Rotations result in variables loading primarily on one factor and having either high or low loadings on a factor and, hence, in many instances, bring about a simplification of the initial solution where variables might have moderate loadings across a number of factors. The simplicity of the rotated factor loading matrix makes for ease of interpretation.

The idea is to find an initial arbitrary solution for the factor loading matrix L such that $LL' = R_c$. Then the unique orthogonal transformation matrix T is found that maximizes the varimax criterion. The

TABLE 8.3
Rotated Factor Loading Matrix for Crime Variables

Variables	Factors	
	1	2
MURDER	0.846	0.328
RAPE	0.434	0.722
ROBBERY	0.845	0.290
ASSAULT	0.710	0.512
BURGLARY	0.389	0.795
THEFT	0.242	0.767
MV THEFT	0.542	0.439
Total Variance explained	2.625	2.389

unique rotated factor loading matrix L_R is then $\underset{(p \times k)}{L} \underset{(k \times k)}{T}$ where k is the number of factors. LT is a solution since $R_c = LT(LT)' = LL'$ since $LT(LT)' = LTT'L'$ and $TT' = I$. The varimax solution is presented in Table 8.3.

Factor 1 has high loadings for violent crimes and relatively low loadings for property crimes. Conversely, the property crimes, burglary and theft, have the highest loadings on Factor 2. However, rape and assault, violent crimes, also have appreciable loadings on this factor so that while we might label this factor, property crimes, it is not as structurally simple as our first factor. Note that whereas Factor 1 explained most of the variance in the unrotated solution, the rotated solution distributes the total variance almost equally between the two rotated factors (Table 8.3). Under circumstances such as this when an orthogonal rotation such as varimax does not result in a clear cut simple structure, some researchers prefer to relax the restriction that the common factors be orthogonal or uncorrelated in order to improve the simple structure of the factor loadings and, hence, the interpretability of the factors. They argue that there is no conceptual reason why factors have to be inherently uncorrelated. Rotations that simplify the structure of the unrotated factor loading matrix but allow for correlated factors are called oblique rotations. There is a tradeoff when using oblique rotations. We are improving the simple structure of the factor loadings at the cost of having to consider, in the interpretation, the correlations among factors. For more details on oblique rotation the reader is referred to Kim and Mueller (1978a, 1978b) or Harman (1976).

9. USES OF PRINCIPAL COMPONENTS IN REGRESSION ANALYSIS

Principal components analysis can be used in regression analysis in a number of ways. If the independent variables are highly correlated, then they can be transformed to principal components and the principal components can be used as the independent variables. If we do not want to transform the independent variables, then principal components can be used indirectly to improve the precision of the regression parameter estimates associated with the independent variables. Principal components analysis can also be used as a diagnostic tool to detect multicollinearities among the independent variables. Multicollinearity means that one or more independent variables are essentially linear combinations of other independent variables. Principal components analysis can also be used to select a subset of independent variables from a larger set.

Regression on Principal Components

If we have a large set of correlated independent variables, then the possibility of transforming the independent variables to principal components should be considered. If the principal components are interpretable, and there are near dependencies (i.e., multicollinearities) among the original independent variables, then there are considerable advantages to be gained. (If the principal components are uninterpretable, then we could rotate the retained components prior to the regression analysis.) If multicollinearity is a problem, then a number of the estimated regression parameters will have large standard errors. The estimated regression parameters associated with the principal components have variances that are proportional to the inverse of the variances of the principal components themselves. Let P be the $n \times p$ matrix of principal component scores, then $P'P$ is the $p \times p$ matrix of the sum of squares and cross products of the principal component scores. Since the principal components are uncorrelated, this will be a diagonal matrix with the sum of squares for the various components as the diagonal elements. The sum of cross products is zero by definition. The sum of squares for the ith principal component is $n\lambda_i$ since the variance of the ith principal component is the ith latent root, λ_i, of R and since we can convert a variance into a sum of squares by multiplying it by its sample size, n. The matrix expression for the variance-covariance of the estimated regression parameters is $\sigma^2(X'X)^{-1}$. For principal components, the matrix corresponding to $(X'X)^{-1}$ is $(P'P)^{-1}$.

The latter matrix is a diagonal matrix with $1/n\lambda_i$ as the p diagonal elements. Thus, the variance of the estimated regression parameter associated with the ith principal component is proportional to $1/n\lambda_i$.

We can easily see from this formula that the estimated regression parameters associated with the large principal components have small standard errors and, conversely, the estimated regression parameters associated with small principal components have large standard errors. If the larger principal components are the most important in predicting a particular dependent variable, then their associated regression parameters will be precisely estimated. However, as Jolliffe (1986) warns, this is not always the case. He presents examples where very small components ($\lambda \leq .10$) are better predictors than much larger components ($\lambda \geq 1$). Another advantage of using principal components as independent variables is that since they are uncorrelated, each regression coefficient can be estimated independently of the other components. That is, the regression coefficient for a particular component remains constant regardless of which other components are either added to or discarded from the model. For correlated independent variables, the regression parameter for a particular variable depends upon which other independent variables are included in the model. The statistical independence of principal components makes it easy to choose the optimal set of predictors of any size. We select those principal components in the order of their correlation with the dependent variable. For example, the best set of size three would contain those principal components with the three highest correlations with the dependent variable.

Principal Components Regression

There may be instances where the variables themselves are of theoretical interest. In this situation, a principal components transformation would be of no direct use. However, if a multicollinearity problem exists, then principal components analysis can be used indirectly to improve the precision of the regression parameter estimates for the original variables. A multicollinearity problem exists if one or more of the latent roots of the correlation (covariance) matrix are very small (e.g., .001). As explained earlier, this means that a linear combination of the independent variables using the elements of the associated latent vector is essentially zero. Consequently, one variable can be nearly expressed as a linear combination of the other variables. This results in large standard errors for the variables involved in these near dependencies. For a further discussion of multicollinearity see Lewis-Beck (1980). We can use the spectral decomposition theorem to substantially reduce the standard errors of the variables associated with multicollinearities. We saw earlier that the correlation matrix R could be decomposed with respect to its latent roots and latent vectors. That is,

$$R = \sum_{i=1}^{p} \lambda_i a_i a_i'.$$

It can be shown that the inverse of the correlation matrix R^{-1} can also be decomposed as

$$\sum_{i=1}^{p} \frac{1}{\lambda_i} a_i a_i'.$$

The latent vector associated with the largest latent root of R is associated with the smallest latent root of R^{-1}, the latent vector associated with the second largest latent root of R is associated with the second smallest latent root of R^{-1} and so on. Since the inverse of $Z'Z$, where Z is an $n \times p$ matrix of standardized variables, is used to compute the variances and covariances of the regression parameter estimates, we need to decompose $(Z'Z)^{-1}$ rather than R^{-1}. Since $Z'Z = nR$, $(Z'Z)^{-1} = (nR)^{-1} = 1/n \ R^{-1}$. The latent vectors of $1/n \ R^{-1}$ are identical to those of R^{-1} and the associated latent roots of $1/n \ R^{-1}$ are proportional to those of R^{-1} where the constant of proportionality is $1/n$ (i.e., the ith latent root of $(Z'Z)^{-1}$ is $1/n\lambda_i$). Thus, $(Z'Z)^{-1}$ can be spectrally decomposed as

$$\sum_{i=1}^{p} \frac{1}{n\lambda_i} a_i a_i'.$$

Since the variance-covariance matrix of the parameter estimates is $\sigma^2(Z'Z)^{-1}$ where σ^2 is the error variance for the regression model, the decomposition of $\sigma^2(Z'Z)^{-1}$ is

$$\sigma^2 \sum_{i=1}^{p} \frac{1}{n\lambda_i} a_i a_i'.$$

From this decomposition we can see that the small principal components make large contributions to the variance-covariance matrix of the regression parameter estimates. They reduce the precision of our regression parameter estimates. In particular, very small principal components reduce the precision of those regression parameter estimates that correspond to large elements in the associated latent vector.

We are usually most interested in the diagonal elements of $\sigma^2(Z'Z)^{-1}$ since they correspond to the variances (or squared standard errors) of the estimated regression parameters. Using this decomposition, we can express the variance of the kth regression parameter as

$$\sigma^2 \sum_{i=1}^{p} \frac{1}{n\lambda_i} a_{ik}^2$$

where a_{ik} is the kth element of the latent vector associated with the ith principal component. We can clearly see that if λ_i is very small and the associated a_{ik} is very large, then the corresponding principal component makes a large contribution to the standard error of the kth regression parameter. If the associated component does not predict the dependent variable, then it seems reasonable to subtract out its substantial contribution to the variance of the kth regression parameter. For example, if the latent root associated with the smallest principal component was very small, then we would drop the last term in the decomposition and use

$$\sigma^2 \sum_{i=1}^{p-1} \frac{1}{n\lambda_i} a_i a_i'$$

as our estimator of the variance-covariance matrix of the regression parameter estimates. If there were two small principal components, then our estimator of the parameter variance-covariance matrix would be

$$\sigma^2 \sum_{i=1}^{p-2} \frac{1}{n\lambda_i} a_i a_i'.$$

If we drop one or more components, then the variance of certain parameter estimates may be substantially reduced. However, some bias may now be introduced into our estimate of the regression parameters, since, in order to be consistent, we must use

$$\sum_{i=1}^{p-k} \frac{1}{n\lambda_i} a_i a_i' Z y'$$

where k is the number of "small" components that have been dropped as our estimator of β, the vector of regression parameters, rather than $(Z'Z)^{-1} Z'y$. If the discarded components are uncorrelated with the dependent variable, then no bias in the regression parameter estimates will result. However, even if they are correlated with the dependent variable, the reduction in the variance of the estimate may more than offset the bias that is introduced.

Example

In order to illustrate the concepts introduced above and to introduce some new concepts, we shall examine a correlation matrix presented in Levine (1977) which in turn was based on data drawn from Taylor and Hudson (1970). The data were originally collected to see if the distribution of expenditures for defense, education, and health could be explained on the basis of six sociodemographic and political characteristics of 58 countries which had data on all characteristics. The six independent variables were population size (POP), population density (DENS), literary rate (LIT), energy consumption per capita (ENERGY), gross national product per capita (GNP/POP), and electoral irregularity score (ELECT). Although there are three dependent variables, we will, for the moment, only consider educational expenditures as a percent of the gross national product (EDUC). The intercorrelations among the seven variables are presented in Table 9.1.

Table 9.1 indicates that all six independent variables have a positive correlation with the dependent variable, educational expenditures (EDUC). LIT, ENERGY, and GNP/POP have high correlations of .610, .640, and .640, respectively, with EDUC. Consequently, regressing EDUC on the six independent variables, should yield a high multiple correlation. Looking at the correlations among the six independent variables we see some high correlations. In particular, ENERGY and GNP/POP have a correlation of .93. We suspect that we might have a multicollinearity problem. Let us look at the results of the regression analysis presented in Table 9.2. The multiple correlation of .689 based on six independent variables is not appreciably higher than the largest single correlation of .64 between either ENERGY or GNP/POP and EDUC. This indicates that the remaining five independent variables do not add much unique variance that is systematically related to EDUC. Even so, the F ratio indicates that the multiple correlation is highly significant ($p < .0005$). While the estimated regression parameters associated with LIT, ENERGY, and GNP/POP are large as we would have expected from their high corre-

70

TABLE 9.1
Correlations Among National Socioeconomic and Political Variables

		1	2	3	4	5	6	7
1	POP	1.000						
2	DENS	0.050	1.000					
3	LIT	0.200	0.450	1.000				
4	ENERGY	0.350	0.230	0.710	1.000			
5	GNP/POP	0.330	0.190	0.740	0.930	1.000		
6	ELECT	0.040	0.320	0.360	0.190	0.360	1.000	
7	EDUC	0.300	0.230	0.610	0.640	0.640	0.170	1.000

TABLE 9.2
Multiple Regression of EDUC on Six Independent Variables

Variable	Regression Parameter Estimate	Standard Error	t ratio	Probability
POP	.101	.109	.925	.360
DENS	.028	.125	.224	.824
LIT	.300	.172	1.747	.087
ENERGY	.161	.322	.501	.619
GNP/POP	.257	.348	.737	.465
ELECT	−.074	.130	−.569	.572

multiple correlation = .689, F-ratio = 7.663 with 6 and 51 degrees of freedom
(p < .0005).

lations with EDUC, none of them are significant at the .05 level. In fact, only LIT even approaches significance. The problem is that while some of the estimated regression parameters are large, so are their standard errors. These regression results are typical of data sets with multicollinearity problems. The overall multiple correlation is highly significant, but all of the estimated regression parameters are insignificant. While various indices of multicollinearity have been proposed in the literature (Dillon and Goldstein, 1984), a rule of thumb is to suspect multicollinearity if the R^2 is highly significant, many of the independent variables have highly significant correlations with the dependent variables, and all, or most, of the multiple regression parameters do not approach statistical significance. If this rule of thumb points towards multicollinearity, then one or more extremely small latent roots of $X'X$ will provide further support.

Let us see how we can apply principal components analysis to address this multicollinearity problem. A principal components analysis of the correlation matrix of the six independent variables is presented in Table 9.3.

The principal components show the typical pattern of the first component reflecting overall size and the remaining components reflecting various contrasts. Table 9.4 presents the correlation of each principal component with the dependent variable, EDUC, and the regression parameter associated with each principal component along with its associated standard error and t ratio.

Except for the standard error of the last coefficient, the standard errors for the principal component regression coefficients are all smaller than the standard errors of the coefficients associated with the original variables. The size of the standard errors are inversely related to the size of the principal components. The largest component has the smallest standard error and the smallest component has the largest standard error. Whereas none of the original estimated regression parameters were statistically significant, the estimated regression parameter associated with the largest principal component was highly significant. While Jolliffe's criteria ($\lambda \geq .70$) would tell us to retain the first four components, for the purpose of predicting ·EDUC we need only retain the first component.

The six principal components together explain exactly the same amount of variance in EDUC as the six original variables. For our transformed parameters, the independence property of principal components allows us to easily select the best subsets with respect to predicting the dependent variable. The best single component subset is the component with the highest correlation with the dependent variable; the best two component subset is comprised of the two components with the highest correlations with the dependent variable, and so on.

If the principal components are difficult to interpret, then the k components with significant correlations with the dependent variable could be rotated to simple structure using varimax or some other rotational procedure. The dependent variable could then be regressed on the rotated components.

Let us suppose that we are not interested in using the principal components as independent variables, but, for conceptual reasons, are interested in the regression parameters associated with the original six independent variables. We saw that we can increase the precision of

TABLE 9.3

Latent Vectors and Roots of the Correlation Matrix of Socioeconomic and Political Variables (N=58)

| Variable | Latent Vector | | | | | |
	1	2	3	4	5	6
POP	.235	−.510	.810	.128	−.108	.005
DENS	.268	.584	.418	−.565	.291	.097
LIT	.503	.113	−.154	−.192	−.817	−.065
ENERGY	.514	−.266	−.242	−.113	.403	−.660
GNP/POP	.529	−.193	−.262	.115	.263	.729
ELECT	.277	.527	.136	.775	.047	−.152
Latent Root	3.036	1.165	.783	.710	.259	.047
Cumulative percent variance explained	50.61	70.02	83.07	94.91	99.21	100

TABLE 9.4

Results from Regressing EDUC on the Six Principal Components

Principal Component	Correlation with EDUC	Regression Coefficient	Standard Error	t ratio
1	.662	.380	.054	7.04 (p < .0001)
2	−.143	−.132	.088	1.50
3	−.061	−.069	.107	.64
4	−.090	−.107	.112	.96
5	−.059	−.116	.118	.98
6	.012	.055	.440	.13

those regression parameter estimates that are involved in near dependencies by deleting the very small principal components that reflect these dependencies. In the present example, there is only one very small latent root, the last root whose value is .047. The latent vector contains two large elements, −.660 for ENERGY and .729 for GNP/POP. The remaining elements are small so that the near dependency can be written as −.660 ENERGY + .729 GNP/POP = 0, or ENERGY = 1.105 GNP/POP. We already noticed the correlation of .93 between ENERGY and GNP/POP so this should not surprise us. Since the elements −.660 and .729 are large and $\lambda = .047$ is small our spectral decomposition of $(Z'Z)^{-1}$ tells us that if we drop this component from the regression equation, the standard errors associated with the ENERGY and GNP/POP regression parameters should be reduced considerably. Besides, we have seen that the smallest component has no value in predicting EDUC. Let us use the decomposition theorem to see how much the standard errors are reduced by discarding the last component and then see how much our parameter estimates have changed because of this deletion.

The contribution of the last component to the variance of the estimated regression coefficient ENERGY is

$$\frac{\hat{\sigma}^2}{n\lambda_6} a_{4,6}^2$$

where $\hat{\sigma}^2$ is the error variance estimate from the regression model. Since we are using standardized variables, $\hat{\sigma}^2$ is estimated as $1 - R^2$ or $1-(.689)^2 = .525$. Substituting the appropriate values in our equation for the contribution of the last component, we have

$$\frac{.525(-.660)^2}{58(.047)} = .084.$$

The regression estimate of the variance associated with this parameter (Table 9.2) was $(.322)^2 = .104$. Subtracting out the contribution of the last component to the variance we have $.104 - .084 = .02$. This is the revised principal components estimate of the variance of the estimated ENERGY regression parameter. We have reduced the variance of our estimate by approximately 80%. Taking the square root of $.02$, our new standard error becomes $.14$. This is considerably smaller than the conventional least squares estimate of $.32$ presented in Table 9.2. Proceeding similarly we find that the contribution of the last principal component to the variance of the estimated regression coefficient for GNP/POP is

$$\frac{\hat{\sigma}^2}{n\lambda_6} a_{5,6}^2 = \frac{.525(.729)^2}{58(.047)} = .102.$$

Subtracting this from the variance of the estimated regression coefficient for GNP/POP, we find $(.348)^2 - .102 = .019$. So our revised standard error becomes $\sqrt{.019} = .138$. We have reduced our standard error from $.348$ to $.138$, the same magnitude of reduction as in the case of ENERGY.

We must also revise our estimates of the regression parameters associated with ENERGY and GNP/POP by subtracting out the contribution of the last principal component to the estimator of β, the estimated vector of regression coefficients. From the previous section, we find that this contribution is

$$\frac{1}{n\lambda_p} a_p a_p' Z y'.$$

Since

$$Zy' = nr_{x,y}$$

where $r_{x,y}$ is the vector of correlations of the independent variables with y, the dependent variable, we can express the contribution of the last component to the regression parameter estimates as

$$\frac{1}{n\lambda_p} a_p a_p' Z y' = \frac{1}{n\lambda_p} a_p a_p' nr_{xy} = \frac{1}{\lambda_p} a_p a_p' r_{xy}$$

for standardized variables. Substituting into this formula, we have

$$\frac{1}{.047} \begin{bmatrix} .005 \\ .097 \\ -.065 \\ -.660 \\ .729 \\ -.152 \end{bmatrix} [.005\ .097\ -.065\ -.660\ .729\ -.152] \begin{bmatrix} .30 \\ .23 \\ .61 \\ .64 \\ .30 \\ .17 \end{bmatrix} = \begin{bmatrix} .01 \\ .01 \\ .02 \\ -.03 \\ .04 \\ -.01 \end{bmatrix}.$$

We can see that the contribution of the last principal component to the values of the estimated regression coefficients is small. Subtracting this vector from the original vector of estimated regression parameters leads to a revised estimator that does not differ appreciably from the original estimator.

Sometimes a very small principal component can have a substantial correlation with the dependent variable (Jolliffe, 1986). Therefore, before we discard one or more very small components we should make sure that their correlation(s) with the dependent variable are small and insignificant. Otherwise, we shall be discarding information that is useful in predicting the dependent variable. Discarding predictive components with very small variances will still reduce the standard errors of the regression coefficients associated with those variables with large weights in the latent vector (i.e., those variables involved in the multicollinearities), but, at the same time, considerable bias will be introduced in our principal components estimators of the regression coefficients associated with the original variables. The bias introduced may more than offset the gains in reducing their standard errors.

10. USING PRINCIPAL COMPONENTS TO DETECT OUTLYING AND INFLUENTIAL OBSERVATIONS

A major advantage of principal components analysis is that if the first two principal components account for a substantial portion of the total variation, then we can approximate the distribution of the observations in the variable space by plotting the principal component scores. This two-dimensional representation of the p-dimensional observations can be used in a number of ways. The plot can be examined for outlying observations, for influential observations, or it can be used to see if the observations can be visually clustered. Outlying observations are observations that lie at a considerable distance from the bulk of the observations or do not conform to the general pattern the observations exhibit. Outlying observations are called influential observations if their deletion from a particular analysis leads to different results (e.g., different parameter estimates in a regression equation or different latent roots and associated latent vectors in a principal components analysis). Outliers, depending on the analysis, do not have to be influential. The use of principal components plots in cluster analysis will be discussed in the next chapter. We presented a plot of the scores for the first two principal components for our state level crime data in Figure 3.7.

Recall that the first two principal components accounted for over 79% of the variation in the seven state level crime variables. So this plot is a good approximation of the distribution of the observations in the original seven-dimensional space. There is nothing unusual about the swarm of points except that Washington, DC, is off by itself in the upper right corner of the plot. It has extreme standardized scores on both principal components. Since all seven crime variables had high loadings or weights on the first component, it might be expected that Washington, DC, had extreme values on one or more of the crime variables. The seven crime scores for the District of Columbia are presented in Table 10.1 along with the means, standard deviations, and other statistics for the total sample of 51 states.

Table 10.1 indicates that Washington, DC, had extremely high values for all seven crime variables. For murder, robbery, assault, and theft it had the maximum sample value. The District of Columbia would have been judged an outlier by looking at its values on the original variables. However, some outliers are picked up by principal component plots that would not be identified by examining their scores one variable at a time. We usually try to find a reason for an observation being an outlier before we decide to delete it from an

TABLE 10.1
Crime Variable Scores for DC and Overall Sample Statistics

Crime	D.C.	Mean	Standard Deviation	Minimum Sample Value	Maximum Sample Value
murder	28.6	6.63	4.56	1.0	28.6
rape	63.7	33.60	15.63	12.9	91.6
robbery	1014.0	147.06	159.17	8.0	1014.0
assault	693.0	253.24	132.25	32.0	693.0
burglary	1767.0	1140.69	374.63	399.0	1978.0
theft	4521.0	2755.39	693.89	1347.0	4521.0
motor vehicle theft	711.0	343.43	194.37	109.0	866.0

analysis. In some cases, the outlying observation could be due to data coding errors and measurement errors. In other cases, it could be due to the special circumstances in which the observation was measured. When we look at the table in the U.S. Statistical Abstracts from which this data was taken, we find a footnote attached to Washington, DC. The footnote indicates the crime rates for the city include offenses reported by the U.S. Park police and Zoological police. Washington, DC, may be somewhat different from other states with respect to the way in which crime statistics are aggregated. Nevertheless, it is quite different from the remaining states and consideration should be given to deleting it from the data set and redoing the principal components analysis to see if the Washington, DC, observation had an influential effect on the results of the analysis.

The latent roots for the first three principal components in the original principal components analysis were 4.71, .837, and .568. With Washington, DC, deleted, the corresponding latent roots were 4.451, .935, and .717. Right away we see that we would have retained a third component in the reduced data set by Jolliffe's criterion. In this sense, it is certainly an influential observation since it changes our representation of the observations from two- to three-dimensions. It reduced the variance of the first component by 5% (i.e., $(4.71 - 4.51)/4.71$) and increased the variance of the second and third components by 12% (i.e., $(.935 - .837)/.837$) and 22% (i.e., $(.717 - .568)/.568$), respectively.

There are also differences between the two analyses in the corresponding elements of the latent vectors, but the interpretation of the first three components in either case is essentially the same. Outliers on the first few PCs are those that typically inflate correlations. For example, Washington, DC, was extremely high on all variables that inflated the correlations among the seven crime variables. When it was removed, the variance of the first component, which reflects the overall size of the correlations, was reduced by 5%. This is a substantial reduction when we realize that only a single observation was removed.

Examining plots of the smallest components is also a worthwhile undertaking. Very small components reflect the correlational structure of the observations since the latent vector associated with a small component indicate, as discussed earlier, how one variable is linearly related to the remaining $p - 1$ variables. An outlier on a small component is an observation that does not fit the correlational structure represented by that component. The direction of the last principal component is orthogonal to the $p - 1$ dimensional subspace defined by the first $p - 1$ principal components. Thus, the first $p - 1$ components are defined by minimizing the sum of squares of the observations in the direction perpendicular to the space defined by the first $p - 1$ principal components. This is the direction of the smallest principal component. Consequently, outliers on the last component are those observations that could influence the directions of the first $p - 1$ components in the space of the p variables.

The scores on the last two principal components were plotted, but not shown here. Texas was identified as a clear outlier in the upper left hand corner of the plot. It appeared to deviate from the correlational structure in the observations represented by the last two components. Like Washington, DC, we can determine how much influence Texas has on our principal components analysis by deleting Texas and redoing the components analysis. A comparison between the principal components results, with and without Texas, showed virtually no differences with respect to both the sizes of the latent roots and the sizes of the corresponding elements in all of the latent vectors. Texas is clearly an outlier, but it is not an influential observation, whereas Washington, DC, was both an outlier and an influential observation since it changed the correlational structure of the crime variables as reflected in the results of the principal components analysis.

Thus, Washington, DC, might also have an influence on the results of a subsequent regression analysis in which the seven crime variables would play the role of independent variables. Therefore, principal components analysis can be used to identify observations that might also be influential observations in other analyses besides principal components analysis.

11. USE OF PRINCIPAL COMPONENTS IN CLUSTER ANALYSIS

If the first two or three principal components account for a substantial proportion of the total variation, as in the state level crime data, then we can also use the plots to visually identify clusters. A cluster is a group of observations that are "closer" to each other than they are to observations in another cluster or group. The plot of the scores on the first two principal components for the crime data does not reveal a clear pattern of clusters. If asked to define three clusters, however, we might come up with the cluster definitions presented in Figure 11.1. They seem to be natural clusters and not arbitrarily defined by a linear partition of the space of the first two principal components. Note that two observations were not included in any of the three clusters. From our definition of the structure of the data in terms of three clusters, we have defined another outlier, New York, in addition to Washington, DC. If asked to define four clusters, we might divide the large cluster into two subclusters. The possibilities are endless unless there are homogeneous clumps of observations with large distances between them.

There are a large number of clustering algorithms that are used to cluster data. For a good discussion of clustering see Aldenderfer and Blashfield (1984). There is no advantage in transforming the original observations to principal component scores prior to the clustering since the same information is contained in the original and the transformed data. That is, for any distance function, the distances among observations computed from principal component scores are equal to the corresponding distances computed from the original variable scores using an equivalent but different distance function.

The only advantage of employing principal components in cluster analysis is to be able to plot the component scores and visually search for clusters of observations as we have done above. Principal components can also be used to verify the clusters determined on the basis of another clustering algorithm. We can see if the previously defined clusters are homogeneous, distinct, and aesthetically appealing to the eye. Clustering algorithms will define clusters even if none exist, i.e., if the observations are evenly spread throughout the variable space. In

FACTOR (1)

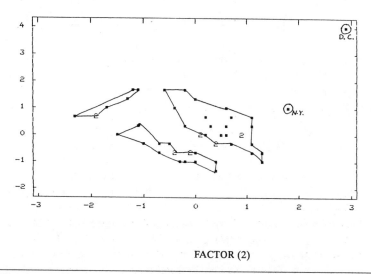

FACTOR (2)

Figure 11.1: Three Clusters of States Defined by Principal Components of Crime Data

this case, the clustering algorithm merely defines an arbitrary partition of the observations into clusters.

Different algorithms lead to both different numbers of clusters and cluster membership with respect to the observations. In fact, the same algorithm when repeated on the same data can sometimes result in a different solution if the rows of the matrix representing the similarity among observations are reordered. For these reasons, a plot of the data on the first two principal components can be informative if they account for a large portion of the total variance. If the data are to be arbitrarily clustered, then visual clustering in the space of the first two principal components is just as good as any other clustering procedure. If the first two principal components do not account for a substantial amount of variation, then it is useful to supplement the plot with information from the third principal component. This can be done in numerous ways. For example, for each plotted point we could represent the score on the third principal component by a minus (–) or plus (+) with the minus sign indicating a high negative score on the third component, the plus sign indicating a high positive score, and a blank (no symbol on the diagram) indicating a score in the middle of the distribution of the third component.

12. USE OF PRINCIPAL COMPONENTS ANALYSIS IN CONJUNCTION WITH OTHER MULTIVARIATE ANALYSIS PROCEDURES

In both linear discriminant function analysis and canonical correlational analysis there is an advantage in transforming the original variables to principal components before undertaking either of these analyses. This is particularly true if the variables are highly correlated and the resulting principal components (or rotated components) have a conceptually appealing interpretation.

Use of Principal Components in Discriminant Analysis

Linear discriminant function analysis is a maximization problem like principal components. It even involves solving for the latent roots and associated latent vectors of a particular matrix. The object of discriminant analysis is to determine one or more linear functions of a set of variables, measured on a number of groups, that maximize the between group variation relative to within group variation on the derived linear composite. In matrix terminology discriminant analysis involves finding a vector of variable weights, a, such that $a'Ba$ is maximized relative to $a'Wa$ where B is the between group sum of squares and cross products matrix and W is the common within group sum of squares and cross products matrix. The solution to this problem involves finding the latent roots and associated latent vectors of the matrix $W^{-1}B$. The number of latent roots (discriminant functions) is equal to the number of groups minus one or the number of variables, whichever is less.

The elements of the latent vector, a_1, associated with the largest latent root, λ_1, are the variable weights associated with the linear discriminant function that maximizes the between to within group variation. The largest latent root, λ_1, is the ratio of the between to within group variation for that linear function. If there are at least three groups or two variables, then there is a second largest latent root, λ_2, and associated vector, a_2 which maximizes the between to within group variation on $a_2'x$ and is uncorrelated with the first discriminant function. The latent root, λ_2, measures the between to within group variation on this second linear discriminant function. Since it is smaller than λ_1, the second orthogonal linear discriminant function has less power to discriminate among groups than the discriminant function associated with the largest root. We continue this process of extracting successively smaller latent roots and associated latent vectors, as in principal components analysis, until all of the between group relative to within group variation is totally accounted for. This occurs, as mentioned above, when we have extracted k linear discriminant functions where k is the lesser of the number of groups minus 1 or the number of variables used to discriminate among the groups. For a further discussion of linear discriminant function analysis see Dunteman (1984b) and Klecka (1980).

If we have a large number of groups and a large number of highly correlated variables, then conducting a discriminant analysis on a subset of the principal components is especially appealing. Since the principal components are uncorrelated, we can test the statistical significance of each one independently of the others by an F ratio associated with a one-way analysis of variance. We can then elect to use only those principal components that individually discriminate between groups. With the original correlated variables, this simple variable selection scheme is not feasible. A variable that alone discriminates among groups, may not add independent discriminatory power when used together with other variables. In most cases, the largest principal components will be the most discriminatory components, but there are always exceptions, as Jolliffe (1986) so forcibly points out. This mainly occurs because a small component is defined primarily by a single variable that adds discriminatory power. For example, Figure 12.1 illustrates a case where the largest principal component does not discriminate among three groups, as well as the second one does. In fact, the second principal component discriminates perfectly among the three groups while the projections of observations on the first principal component would show considerable overlap.

Example

Let us return to our crime data where the 51 states can be subdivided into 9 geographical regions. We can use the principal component scores, rather than the original variables, to conduct a discriminant analysis. Since the seven principal components are statistically independent, each one makes an independent contribution with respect to discriminating among the nine regions. We can thus conduct a one-way analysis of variance for each principal component with regions as the categorical independent variable and the particular principal component score as the dependent variable. The seven analysis of variances indicate that only principal components two and three are statistically significant. The F ratios were 6.623 and 6.253,

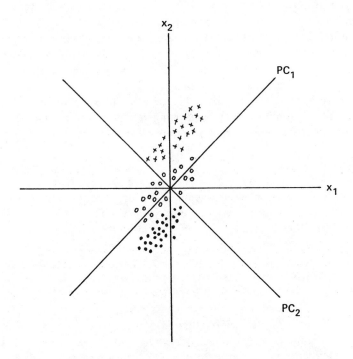

Figure 12.1: Distribution of Groups on the First Two Principal Components

respectively, and with 8 and 42 degrees of freedom each one was highly significant ($p < .0001$).

The F ratio associated with the largest principal component was not significant at the .05 level although it approached significance. By itself, the largest principal component, although accounting for over 67% of the total variation in the seven crime variables, did not significantly discriminant among the nine regions. We noted that this largest principal component reflected overall crime level. Thus, regions don't differ very much with respect to overall crime level, but differ with respect to patterns of crime which are represented by the second and third components. We previously interpreted the second principal component as a contrast between violent personal crimes and property crimes. Since the third component had a latent root less than .70 (.57) we did not interpret it. It seems to be primarily defined by motor vehicle theft. We see the danger of arbitrarily discarding principal components if they are to be used in subsequent analyses. If we only retained the first two principal components, then we would have included one component, the first, that was relatively useless in discriminating among the nine regions and rejected one, the third, which exhibited extremely high discriminatory power.

The discriminant analysis indicated that only the first two discriminant functions were statistically significant. Both were highly significant at the .0001 level. The canonical correlations associated with these two discriminant functions were .819 and .801, respectively. These correlations indicate a high association between the regions and each of the two discriminant functions. The canonical correlations are identical to those that would have been obtained if we had used the seven original crime variables since the seven principal components completely account for the variation in the seven crime variables.

Let us now examine the vector of weights shown in Table 12.1 for these two discriminant functions. The weights are for the principal component scores after these each have been standardized to have a within region standard deviation of 1. Principal component 3 has by far the largest weight on the first discriminant function, and likewise, the second principal component has the largest weight, by far, on the second discriminant function. The results are consistent with the univariate F ratios discussed above. Let us see how well we can do by using these two principal components alone with respect to discriminating among the nine regions. We can do this by conducting a linear discriminant function analysis with only components 2 and 3 and comparing the canonical correlations derived from this analysis with those from the discriminant analysis discussed above which used the information in all seven crime variables. Since there are only two variables and nine regions, all of the between region differences are captured by two linear discriminant functions. Both of the discriminant functions were highly significant (p < .0001). The standardized weights and canonical correlations are presented in Table 12.2. The second principal component essentially defines discriminant function 1 and the third principal component essentially defines discriminant function 2. The two canonical correlations are high, .752 and .732, respectively, indicating strong associations between the geographical regions and the second and third principal components.

If we take the ratio of the corresponding squared canonical correlations for each of the two discriminant functions, putting the smaller one on top, this gives us the proportion of discriminatory power that the two-component linear discriminant function has in comparison with the full seven component discriminant analysis. The ratios are

TABLE 12.1
Standardized Linear Discriminant Function Weights for
Crime by Region Data

Principal Component	Discriminant Function	
	1	2
1	.252	−.457
2	.269	.978
3	.911	−.234
4	.539	.165
5	−.345	−.222
6	.309	.118
7	−.514	.283
canonical correlation	.819	.801

TABLE 12.2
Standardized Linear Discriminant Function Weights for Components
Two and Three Analysis

Principal Component	Discriminant Function	
	1	2
2	.873	−.489
3	.513	.859
canonical correlation	.752	.732

$$\frac{(.752)^2}{(.819)^2} = .84 \text{ and } \frac{(.732)^2}{(.801)^2} = .84,$$

respectively. These high ratios indicate that most of the discriminatory information resides in just components two and three. The dimensions that discriminate among regions are violent personal crimes versus property crimes and motor vehicle thefts.

Some researchers prefer to use the pooled within group covariance or correlation matrix to determine the principal components for a discriminant analysis rather than using the total correlation matrix as we did. The preference depends on whether we want to emphasize the within group characteristics of the discriminant function or emphasize the discriminatory structure of the data as a whole. Depending on the pattern of differences among the groups, the pooled within group correlation matrix can differ considerably from the total correlation matrix.

If between group differences on the variates are large relative to within group variation, then the largest principal components will be oriented in the direction of between group differences. On the other hand, the largest principal components of the pooled within groups covariance matrix, in this case, are not necessarily those that account for a significant proportion of between group variation. Using the principal components from the pooled within group covariance matrix does, however, allow us to determine if the same principal components that account for most of the within group variation account for most of the between group differences. If the separate within group covariance matrices differ from one another, then pooling is not justified in the first place. In this instance, it makes more sense to either use the principal components of the total covariance matrix or use a nonlinear discriminant analysis where information concerning the differences in the covariance matrices is used to discriminate among groups. The choice is somewhat arbitrary in that the total set of principal components generated by either approach will completely account for between group differences.

The discriminant analysis can be done using both approaches and the choice of one approach over the other can be based upon factors such as the interpretability of the resulting principal components, the number of principal components required for adequately discriminating among groups, and whether or not it is the largest or smallest components that are discriminating among the groups. If the between group variation on the variables is not large relative to within group variation, then either approach will yield essentially the same results.

A principal component analysis of the pooled within groups correlation matrix, for our crime data, not presented here because of space limitations, showed a strong similarity to the principal components for the total correlation matrix which we used in our discriminant analysis. So, in this instance, either choice yields the same results.

Use of Principal Components in Canonical Correlation Analysis

Canonical correlation analysis, originated by Hotelling (1935), involves partitioning a set of variables into two subsets and finding pairs of linear composites, one composite representing each variable set, that are maximally correlated. The variables are often partitioned into a set of independent and dependent variables, although canonical correlation analysis makes no assumptions about the direction of causality; each of the two variable sets is given equal status. Canonical correlation analysis has conceptual similarities to both principal components and discriminant analysis. If the set of p variables is divided into two subsets of p_1 and p_2 variables with $p_1 \leq p_2$, then we can solve for p_1 pairs of linear composites where each pair of composites has the maximum correlation and is uncorrelated with the linear composites making up the other pairs. For example, the largest canonical correlation is obtained by finding the pair of weight vectors $[a_{11}, a_{12}, \ldots, a_{1p}]$ and $[b_{11}, b_{12}, \ldots, b_{1p}]$ such that the correlation between

$$\sum_{i=1}^{p_1} a_{1i} x_i \text{ and } \sum_{i=1}^{p_2} b_{1i} y_i$$

is maximized. This involves finding the largest latent root and associated latent vectors of matrix products involving the within subset and between subset correlation matrices and their inverses. Like principal components analysis and discriminant analysis, we can continue solving for canonical correlations and their associated weighting vectors until all of the independent linear relationships between the two variable sets are accounted for. For more details the reader is referred to Mardia, Kent, and Bibby (1979), Levine (1977), and Thompson (1984).

Rather than using the original variables for the canonical correlation analysis, we can, as we did in our discriminant analysis example, transform the original variables into principal components before conducting the canonical correlation analysis. In this case, we would conduct a principal components analysis within each of the two variable sets and use the principal components rather than the original variables in the canonical correlation analysis. Once again, the advantage is simplicity and interpretability. This is especially true if the number of large principal components within each variable set are relatively small and turn out to have high loadings (correlations) on their respective canonical variates. In this situation, the analysis would indicate that the dimensions that account for most of the variation within variable sets are also important in determining relationships across variable sets. An obvious advantage is that we would have less canonical loadings to interpret.

Another approach would be to conduct a single principal components analysis on the total set of variables. We can then see which components reflect mainly the structure of the data within each of the variable sets and which components explain significant variation across both variable sets. The reason for conducting a principal components analysis on the total set of variables, keeping in mind the distinction between the two variable sets when interpreting the principal components, is that canonical correlation analysis has some serious shortcomings due to its singular focus on maximizing the correlation between linear composites across the variable sets. Specifically, while a linear composite (canonical variate) from one variable set may correlate highly with the corresponding canonical variate from the other data set, the correlation of each variable with its corresponding canonical variate may be low, indicating that each canonical variate explains little of the variation in the individual variables within its respective variable set. Furthermore, each canonical variate from one variable set may not explain much of the variation in the individual variables from the other variable set. Principal components analysis helps balance the objectives of finding both dimensions that explain variation across both data sets and dimensions that explain variation primarily within one data set or the other. For example, if two variable sets are highly related, then one or more large principal components will have substantial loadings from both variable sets. Other principal components, hopefully, the smaller ones, will be defined primarily by one variable set or the other.

13. OTHER TECHNIQUES RELATED TO PRINCIPAL COMPONENTS

Principal Coordinate Analysis

We have seen that we can decompose a covariance or correlation matrix in terms of its latent roots and latent vectors. That is,

$$R = \lambda_1 a_1 a_1' + \lambda_2 a_2 a_2' + \ldots + \lambda_p a_p a_p' = \sum_{i=1}^{p} \lambda_i a_i a_i'.$$

Principal coordinate analysis (Gower, 1966) involves decomposing an $n \times n$ similarity matrix in the same manner. Instead of decomposing a $p \times p$ correlation or covariance matrix of variables, we decompose an $n \times n$ matrix whose elements are measures of similarity between all pairs of observations. The correlation or covariance matrix summarizes the similarity among the p variables rather than the n observations. The similarity measures can be of any type as long as the $n \times n$

similarity matrix, S, is positive-semidefinite and symmetrical like a correlation matrix. Positive-semidefinite means that there are no negative latent roots.

If the matrix S fulfills the two conditions, then we can use the spectral decomposition theorem to decompose S in terms of its latent roots and latent vectors. That is,

$$S = \lambda_1 a_1 a_1' + \lambda_2 a_2 a_2' + \ldots + \lambda_n a_n a_n' = \sum_{i=1}^{n} \lambda_i a_i a_i'.$$

If we let $b_i = \sqrt{\lambda_i}\, a_i$, then the decomposition of S can be written as

$$S = \sum_{i=1}^{n} b_i b_i'.$$

If we consider the n observations as points in n-dimensional space, then the vector b_1 contains the coordinates of the n observations on the first dimension, b_2 contains the coordinates on the second dimension, and so on through b_n which contains the coordinates of the n observations on the nth dimension.

The first stage of principal coordinate analysis is to solve for the b_i. The second and final stage of principal coordinate analysis is to treat the n b_i vectors as the data set (i.e., $[b_1 b_2 \ldots b_n]$) and conduct a principal component analysis on this data set. We can then plot the principal component scores with respect to the first k principal components where k is determined by the same criteria as discussed earlier and used throughout this book.

Gower (1966) points out that principal coordinate analysis and principal components analysis are equivalent if the similarity measure is proportional to Euclidean distance. It turns out that two widely used similarity measures are proportional to Euclidean distance. The first of these two similarity measures is the covariance or correlation between the observations. In this case, S is an $n \times n$ matrix of covariances or correlations among observations rather than variables. We then use this particular S as our starting point for the two steps in our principal coordinate analysis. The second widely used similarity measure is applicable to binary data. It is sometimes called a matching coefficient. This similarity measure is the proportion of the p variables that take the same value for any pair of individuals or observations. Binary variables take only two values, by most conventions, 0 or 1. The similarity between the jth and kth individual or observation is simply the number of times that the patterns 0,0 or 1,1 occur divided by the total number of variables. The patterns 0,0 and 1,1 are matches while the patterns 1,0 or 0,1 are mismatches. The matching similarity coefficient is equivalent to a Euclidean distance measure.

It should be emphasized that if the similarity measure is not proportional to Euclidean distance then principal coordinate analysis and principal component analysis do not produce equivalent results. Principal coordinate analysis is most useful when we do not have measures for p variables on n observations that are required for principal components analysis, but instead have only the similarity measures among the n observations. The latter situation occurs, for example, if we have people rate the similarity between pairs of objects or people with respect to a set of attributes. The aims of principal coordinate analysis in this case are to determine the number of dimensions people use to judge similarity among a particular set of objects or people and to plot the scores for the objects or people in a, hopefully, low dimensional space. If we have the $n \times p$ data matrix, then we might as well do a principal components analysis to begin with unless we want to use this $n \times p$ data matrix to create an $n \times n$ similarity matrix containing non-Euclidean similarity measures. In any event, principal components and principal coordinate analysis have similar goals, to reduce dimensionality, and rely on the spectral decomposition theorem to decompose their respective matrices in terms of their latent roots and latent vectors.

Correspondence Analysis

Correspondence analysis is another multivariate technique related to principal components analysis. Its goal is to summarize the information in a two-way contingency table with r rows and c columns. Our previous applications of principal components analysis were focused on n by p data matrices where p variables were measured on n individuals or observations. The goal was to transform the $n \times p$ matrix to an $n \times k$ matrix of principal component scores where k was considerably less than p. In correspondence analysis we deal with two categorical variables (e.g., geographical region, sex, ethnicity, type of community, etc.) that are crossed to define cells for which frequencies are available from a sample of observations.

We can consider the rows of the contingency table as observations and the columns of the table as variables and conduct a principal components analysis of a transformation of the contingency table in order to generate principal component score vectors for the rows. We also want to generate principal component scores summarizing information in the columns of the contingency table. We do this by transposing the transformed contingency table so that the columns are now rows and conducting a principal components analysis of this matrix in order to generate the scores associated with columns. We usually only generate the scores associated with the two largest principal components associated with the transformed contingency table and its transpose. This is because we usually want to plot the scores associated with the rows and columns of the transformed contingency table in a two dimensional figure so that we see the correspondence between row and column scores.

Jolliffe (1986) used correspondence analysis on a contingency table where a large number of bird species were cross classified with a large number of geographical sites. The rows (bird species) and columns (sites) of the contingency table were each summarized by two dimensions. Jolliffe then plotted in the two dimensional space the scores for bird species and the scores for the geographical areas, which were wetland sites in Ireland. The plot of the pair of r scores for species and the pair of c scores for sites in the two dimensional space was informative in two respects. Species that are close to each other in the two dimensional space are similar to each other with respect to their original data. The same holds for sites. Second, it indicated which species tended to inhabit which sites. A species that is near a particular site in the two dimensional plot indicates that the species is likely to inhabit that site.

An application of correspondence analysis for social scientists might be to summarize the data in a contingency table cross classifying different types of drug abuse treatment programs with client types. Drug treatment programs (e.g., outpatient drug free as one category) could be considered the row variable with r categories and client type (e.g., young, black, females as one category) could be considered the column variable with c columns. This $r \times c$ contingency table would contain, for a sample of n observations, the distribution of the observations across the r times c cells. The outcome of the correspondence analysis would be a set of scores for the rows of the table which represent treatments and a set of scores for the columns which represent client types.

We would retain only two scores representing the r treatment programs and only two scores representing the c client types so that the scores for both treatment programs and client types could be plotted in the same two dimensional space. Since there are r treatments, there would be r values for each of the two score distributions characterizing treatments. Similarly, since there are c client types, there would be c values for each of the two score distributions characterizing client types. If we plot the treatment scores and the client type scores in the same two dimensional space, then we can see if treatments or client types form clusters and, more importantly, if certain treatments and client types occupy the common regions of the two dimensional space which would indicate a correspondence between treatment and client types. That is, we can determine which treatments certain types of clients are more likely to enter.

Correspondence analysis involves, as mentioned above, first transforming the contingency table which, for a data set of n observations, contains the number of observations falling into each of the cells defined by the intersection of a particular row and column. The number of observations falling into the cell defined by the ith row and jth column is denoted as n_{ij}. The first step in the transformation is to divide each cell frequency, n_{ij}, by n to convert the cell counts into probabilities, p_{ij}. In analyzing a contingency table, we are interested in the association between the row and column variable. If the two variables are independent, then each cell probability, p_{ij}, is equal to the product of the corresponding row and column marginal probabilities which are denoted by p_i and p_j, respectively. That is, if the two variables are independent, then $p_{ij} - p_i p_j = 0$ for all i and j. If the two variables are not independent, the $p_{ij} - p_i p_j$ take a nonzero value for some values of i and j. The $p_{ij} - p_i p_j$ can be considered as residuals under the model of independence. If the two categorical variables are highly related, then some of these residuals will be large. This indicates that the model of independence does not fit the data in the contingency table very well. Correspondence analysis focuses on these residuals rather than the original cell probabilities. Its goal is to summarize the pattern of residuals by generating scores associated with rows and scores associated with columns. Note that for a regular $n \times p$ data set, we do not usually do a principal components analysis on the raw data matrix, but first subtract out the mean for each variable. We are interested in summarizing patterns of deviations from the mean.

Correspondence analysis involves yet another transformation on the residuals $p_{ij} - p_i p_j$. Each residual is divided by the product of the square root of the associated marginal probabilities. That is, the new cell entries become

$$\frac{p_{ij} - p_i p_j}{\sqrt{p_i} \sqrt{p_j}} .$$

This last step in the transformation adjusts the residuals with respect to the size of the marginal probabilities. This is similar to standardizing a deviation score cross product by dividing it by the product of the standard deviations. Our transformation is now complete.

The next step is to conduct two principal components analyses on the $r \times c$ matrix with the transformed cell entries. The first principal components analysis considers the rows as observations and the columns as variables and, hence, generates score vectors associated with rows. The second principal components analysis is conducted on the transpose of the transformed data matrix so that now the columns are treated as observations in the analysis and score vectors can be generated for columns. The scores associated with the largest two principal components for each analysis are then plotted so that clusters can be identified and, more importantly, correspondences between the row and column variables can be visually identified.

In a sense, correspondence analysis is a graphical procedure for clustering both the row categories (with respect to the column categories) and the column categories (with respect to the row categories). Both row categories and column categories are represented by scores from their respective two largest principal components so that the information can be plotted in two dimensions. Obviously, correspondence analysis is most useful when both the number of row and column categories are large. Otherwise, we could "see" the similarity between rows or between columns by directly examining the contingency table. The reader desiring more details or further applications is referred to Greenacre (1984).

14. SUMMARY AND CONCLUSIONS

Principal components analysis is useful in significantly reducing the dimensionality of a data set characterized by a large number of correlated variables. Many times the principal components have a natural interpretation; if not, they can be rotated. The principal component scores can be plotted to identify clusters of observations as well as outlying and influential observations. In general, principal components analysis helps us understand the structure of a multivariate data set. If we do not want to transform our original variables to principal components, principal components analysis can still be useful in selecting a small subset of variables that contains most of the statistical information in the much larger original set of variables.

In addition, principal components analysis is useful when used in conjunction with other multivariate procedures. It addresses the multicollinearity problem in multiple regression analysis. Multicollinearity is evidenced by the presence of principal components with extremely small variances. This shows that both large and small variance principal components are useful in understanding the structure of a data set. In some cases, the substitution of a few principal components for the original variables can enhance our understanding of a linear discriminant function analysis or a canonical correlation analysis. In fact, all three procedures involve finding linear composites that maximize a particular criterion. The procedure is so fundamental that it is closely related to other techniques that appear, on the surface, to be quite different. We have seen, for example, its relationship to principal coordinate analysis and its use in analyzing contingency table data by correspondence analysis. The reader who is interested in further details on principal components analysis presented in a more rigorous fashion is referred to the excellent book by Jolliffe (1986).

We will conclude with a word of caution. It makes no sense to conduct a principal components analysis on a hodge podge of variables that have low intercorrelations. It will take nearly as many principal components as there are original variables to account for a major portion of variance in the original variables. If we rotated these components we would find ourselves back to where we started in the sense that most of the rotated components will be defined essentially by a single variable.

REFERENCES

ALDENDERFER, M. S., & BLASHFIELD, R. K. (1984). Cluster Analysis. Beverly Hills, CA: Sage.

ANDERSON, T. W. (1963). "Asymptotic theory for principal components analysis." Annuals of Mathematical Statistics, 34: 122-148.

BIRREN, J. E., & MORRISON, D. F. (1961). "Analysis of WAIS subtests in relation to age and education." Journal of Gerontology, 16: 363-369.

CATTELL, R. B. (1966). "The scree test for the number of factors." Multivariate Behavioral Research, 1: 245-276.

DILLON, R., & GOLDSTEIN, M. (1984). Multivariate analysis: Methods and applications. New York: John Wiley.

DUNTEMAN, G. H. (1984a). Introduction to linear models. Beverly Hills, CA: Sage.

DUNTEMAN, G. H. (1984b). Introduction to multivariate analysis. Beverly Hills, CA: Sage.

GOWER, J. C. (1966). Some distance properties of latent root and vector methods used in multivariate analysis. Biometrika, 53: 325-328.

GREENACRE, M. J. (1984). Theory and applications of correspondence analysis. London: Academic Press.

GUTTMAN, L. (1956). "Best possible systematic estimates of communalities." Psychometrika, 21: 273-285.

HARMAN, H. H. (1976). Modern factor analysis. Chicago: University of Chicago Press.

HOTELLING, H. (1933). "Analysis of a complex of statistical variables into principal components." Journal of Educational Psychology, 24: 417-441, 498-520.

HOTELLING, H. (1935). "The most predictable criterion." Journal of Educational Psychology, 26: 139-142.

JOLLIFFE, I. T. (1972). "Discarding variables in a principal component analysis, I: Artificial data." Applied Statistics, 21: 160-173.

JOLLIFFE, I. T. (1986). Principal component analysis. New York: Springer-Verlag.

KAISER, H. F. (1958). "The varimax criterion for analytic rotation in factor analysis." Psychometrika, 23: 187-200.

KAISER, H. F. (1960). "The application of electronic computers to factor analysis." Educational and Psychological Measurement, 20: 141-151.

KIM, J., & MUELLER, C. W. (1978a). Introduction to factor analysis. Beverly Hills, CA: Sage.

KIM, J., & MUELLER, C. W. (1978b). Factor analysis. Beverly Hills, CA: Sage.

KLECKA, W. R. (1980). Discriminant analysis. Beverly Hills, CA: Sage.

LAWLEY, D. N. (1963). "On testing a set of correlation coefficients for equality." Annuals of Mathematical Statistics, 34: 149-151.

LAWLEY, D. N., & Maxwell, A. E. (1971). Factor analysis as a statistical method. New York: American Elsevier.

LEVINE, M. S. (1977). Canonical analysis and factor comparison. Beverly Hills, CA: Sage.

LEWIS-BECK, M. (1980). Applied regression: An introduction. Beverly Hills, CA: Sage.

LONG, J. S. (1983). Confirmatory factor analysis. Beverly Hills, CA: Sage.

MARDIA, K. V., KENT, J. T., & BIBBY, J. M. (1979). Multivariate analysis. London: Academic Press.

McCABE, G. P. (1984). "Principal variables." Technometrics, 26: 137-144.

MORRISON, D. F. (1976). Multivariate statistical methods (2nd ed.). New York: McGraw-Hill.

NAMBOODIRI, K. (1984). Matrix algebra: An introduction. Beverly Hills, CA: Sage.

PEARSON, K. (1901). On lines and planes of closest fit to systems of points in space. Phil., May 2:559-572.

Statistical Abstracts of the United States (1985). Washington, DC: U.S. Department of Commerce, Bureau of Census.

TAYLOR, C. L., & HUDSON, M. C. (1972). World handbook of social and political indicators (2nd ed.). New Haven, CT: Yale University Press.

THOMPSON, R. (1984). Canonical correlation analysis: Uses and interpretation. Beverly Hills, CA: Sage.

THURSTONE, L. L. (1947). Multiple factor analysis. Chicago: University of Chicago Press.

WILKINSON, L. (1986). SYSTAT: The system for statistics. Evanston, IL: SYSTAT.

WOODWARD, J. A., RETKA, R. L., & NG, L. (1984). "Construct validity of heroin abuse estimators." International Journal of the Addictions, 19: 93-117.

GEORGE H. DUNTEMAN is currently Chief Scientist at the Research Triangle Institute, where he is actively involved in applied research, primarily in the social and behavioral sciences. He has previously held research appointments at the Educational Testing Service and the U.S. Army Research Institute. He has also held assistant and associate professorships at the University of Rochester and the University of Florida, respectively. During the 1987–1988 academic year he was a Visiting Professor of Management in the Babcock School of Management at Wake Forest University where he taught the MBA core course in quantitative methods. Dr. Dunteman received his Ph.D. from Louisiana State University in industrial/organizational psychology with a minor in industrial engineering. He also has an M.S. degree from Iowa State University with a major in industrial psychology and a minor in statistics. His B.A. degree from St. Lawrence University is in sociology. He is currently on the editorial board of Educational and Psychological Measurement and had published widely in professional journals. He previously authored two books for Sage—Introduction to Linear Models (1984) and its companion volume, Introduction to Multivariate Analysis (1984).

Quantitative Applications
in the Social Sciences

A SAGE UNIVERSITY PAPERS SERIES

$9.95 each

SAGE PUBLICATIONS, INC.
P.O. BOX 5084
THOUSAND OAKS, CALIFORNIA 91359-9924

Place
Stamp
here